HISTORIC
WINDSOR

GARTH VAUGHAN

NIMBUS
PUBLISHING

Dedication

This book is dedicated to my parents, James "Jimmy" and Olive "Ollie" Vaughan, and three dear friends of theirs and mine, H. Carleton "Ky" Smith, Katherine "Kay" Anslow and Peter "Pete" MacKinnon. Each played an important part in stimulating my interest in the local history of Windsor, a subject that was not included in our school curriculum, but which became my lifetime interest.

Any of the five could easily have prepared such a book as this. I am honored to carry on where they left off and show these photos and relate stories as they would have done.

Nimbus Publishing Limited
PO Box 9166
Halifax, NS B3K 5M8
(902) 455-4286

Printed and bound in Canada
Design: Margaret Issenman, MGDC
Front cover: Heather Bryan

Library and Archives Canada Cataloguing in Publication

Vaughan, Garth
Historic Windsor / Garth Vaughan.
Includes bibliographical references.
ISBN 1-55109-560-2

1. Windsor (N.S.)—History. 2. Windsor (N.S.)—History—Pictorial works. I. Title.
FC2349.W5V38 2006   971.6'35   C2006-901494-9

Canadä   The Canada Council | Le Conseil des Arts
for the Arts | du Canada

We acknowledge the financial support of the Government of Canada through the Book Publishing Industry Development Program (BPIDP) and the Canada Council, and of the Province of Nova Scotia through the Department of Tourism, Culture and Heritage for our publishing activities.

Contents

Introduction

The town of Windsor, Nova Scotia, is one of the most historically significant places in the province. It was a centre of culture, leisure, and higher education long before the provincial capital, Halifax, and its historical importance in the world of sport is uncontested.

Situated at the junction of the Avon and Saint Croix rivers, which flow into the Minas Basin and on into the Bay of Fundy, the town is centrally located. The area was inhabited by Mi'kmaq for centuries before any European settlers arrived; the two rivers supplied an abundance of seafood in the spring, summer, and autumn. Cod, salmon, shad, gaspereau, flounder, eels, and smelts poured in from the Bay of Fundy. Ducks and geese filled the air, and deer, moose, and rabbits inhabited the woodland in great numbers, providing protein and fat for fall and winter months. The Mi'kmaq built *wikuom* (wigwams) on the shores of the rivers and in the woods, and were able to sustain themselves in all seasons. They named the area "Pesegitk," which, according to Silas Rand's 1888 *Dictionary of the Language of the Micmac Indians,* means "to flow splitwise." The tidal water that flows in from the ocean through Minas Basin does indeed flow splitwise, into the Avon and St. Croix rivers.

French explorers, led by Samuel de Champlain, began to explore the Bay of Fundy in 1604, and the first French settlers arrived in what later became the Windsor area around 1684. Soon known as Acadians, they built dykes along riverbanks to reclaim marsh areas as agricultural land. They apparently had difficulty pronouncing the word "Pesegitk," and it is generally understood that they pronounced and spelled it "Piziquid."

The next group to arrive in the area were the English. They quickly settled the area as a defensive move, and constructed Fort Edward to guard against attacks by Acadians and Mi'kmaq.

By 1755 the English in Nova Scotia had decided that the peaceful Acadians were a threat to the security of the British presence—the Acadians, although they had sworn allegiance to the English King in 1729, now refused to give a non-conditional oath of allegiance;

Titles of Windsor Throughout its History

- Centre of Culture and Learning

- Playground of Halifax

- Athens of Nova Scotia

- Shiretown of Hants County

- Birthplace of Ice Hurley/Ice Hockey

- Gateway to the Valley

- World-renowned Port of Registry

- Canada's Third-largest Port

- World's Highest Tides

they were determined not to take up arms against either the French or the English. They were deported from the lands that they had made fertile, separated from their communities and often their families, and sent to destinations near and far.

That led to the arrival of the Planters, who came by invitation from the New England colonies to settle the lands formerly belonging to the Mi'kmaq and Acadian families. Loyalists, among them a significant number of black people, arrived a decade later following the American War of Independence. In the years immediately following, groups of immigrants from England, Scotland, and Ireland arrived to begin new lives on grants of land in Britain's newest colony.

In 1764, the Township of Windsor was created, and it was incorporated as a town in 1878. From its inception, it was a place of culture, sport, and society. Wealthy Haligonians looking to escape the city, which was for a long time not much more than a military garrison, came to highbrow, comfortable Windsor. The town became known as the "Playground of Halifax."

Windsor and its surroundings offered excellent hunting of wild game and birds, as well as trout and salmon fishing in its lakes and streams. Horse racing was established at a track at the base of Fort Edward in 1765—the first in English Canada. King's College School was established in Windsor in 1788, creating an even more sophisticated atmosphere in the town. Field sports were quickly organized, and cricket, widely considered "the gentlemen's game," was introduced to King's College in the 1840s by Charles Bowman, a Windsor native and King's student who had also attended school in England and returned with the necessary equipment. The Three Elms Cricket Club was formed, attracting a Halifax Garrison team as well. Renowned writer Thomas Chandler Haliburton reminds us that "rounders," as he referred to it, was played at the King's Collegiate as well; it eventually became baseball in New York.

Windsor is the Little Town of Big Firsts! The town boasts the first...

- Export of gypsum to American ports: 1760s
- Agricultural fair in North America: 1765
- Horseracing in English Canada: 1765
- College School in Canada (King's College School): 1788
- College in Canada (King's College granted Royal Charter): 1790
- Bachelor of Arts degree in Canada: 1790
- Bachelor of Theology degree in Canada: 1790
- Library and Reading Society in Canada: 1790
- Hurley on ice (which became ice hockey): c.1800
- Branch Bank of Nova Scotia: 1837
- Covered bridge in Nova Scotia (Sangster's bridge, at Upper Falmouth): 1802
- Stagecoach line in the Maritimes (Halifax to Windsor): 1816
- Canadian author to gain international recognition (T. C. Haliburton): 1830
- Cricket played in Nova Scotia (at King's College): 1840
- Public railway in Nova Scotia (Halifax to Windsor): 1858
- Town in Canada to have a covered ice rink: 1870
- Telephones in Nova Scotia (at King's College): 1872
- Nova Scotian schooner named *Bluenose*: 1903

The sport for which Windsor is most famous emerged near the year 1800. Hurley, an Irish form of field hockey, was being played by immigrants in Nova Scotia, and many students in Windsor took to the game. It developed into "hurley on the ice," which eventually became ice hockey. Skating had long been popular in Windsor, where there were a host of good ponds to provide ice surfaces for all "skatists" and, later, "hockeyists," the largest and best of which was Long Pond, bigger than three modern-day NHL arena ice surfaces put together!

Of course, the sports and leisure activities available in Windsor were maintained because the town thrived economically. Much of its early economic success depended on its natural resources and its viability as a shipping port. The early discovery of great deposits of gypsum and lime in Windsor and the surrounding countryside led to an export industry to New England as early as the 1770s. In 1800, Neil McGeachy and John Clarke, Windsor landowners also involved in quarrying gypsum, sought permission from the governing council of the colony to build a wharf on the Avon River shore at Windsor. The waterfront continued to develop from there, and ships began to be built at villages along the shores of the Avon, especially at Windsor, which by 1836 was a world-renowned centre of shipping. Between 1840 and 1890 the teeming port's volume of goods shipped was third only to Montreal and Saint John.

Travel between Halifax, Saint John, Boston, and New York was only by sea in those early years, and many travellers to and from Halifax made their connections at Windsor. Fine hotels such as the Avon, Clifton, Victoria, Dufferin, Pellow's, or Pool's catered to travellers waiting to make connections with stagecoach, train, or ship, and teams of fine horses at three livery stables transported people to and from trains and ships as well as regional destinations.

Many local businesses took advantage of the burgeoning shipping industry. The Windsor Foundry was created for the purpose of making iron parts for wooden ships, but before long it was also exporting Windsor and Acorn brand stoves to homes and businesses near and far. And lumber, needed for the great building boom in

CHILDREN ON CHAPEL HILL, 1896

the colony following the establishment of English rule, was plentiful in the Windsor area and swelled the export business. Shiploads of "pit-props," which supported the roofs of coal and gold mines, were sent to mining industries around the world.

In the 1890s, sail gave way to steam and wooden ships gave way to those of iron and steel, and Windsor's shipbuilding industry came to an end. However, as the town lost one industry, local entrepreneurs created others. The plentiful supply of lumber gave rise to the Windsor Furniture Factory, which supplied high-quality home and office furniture to the surrounding area and eventually the rest of Canada. The Annapolis Valley apple industry thrived because of high demand in Britain. Farmers experienced bumper crops, and apple storage warehouses popped up along the developing railway lines. Thousands of barrels were shipped from the government wharf in Windsor up until the time of World War Two. The Colonial Fertilizer Company created fertilizer for farming from local lime quarries and exported it to the world market by shiploads from its own commercial wharf. At the same time, the Nova Scotia Cotton Company (now Nova Scotia Textiles Ltd.) became famous for high-quality cotton goods, and the shipping of gypsum to the hungry American building market increased. Then, as rail and road became the preferred way of shipping most goods, Windsor's waterfront shipping came to an end. The town council missed out on the opportunity to attract a major shipping centre for gypsum, the one product still exported by sea; that contract went to the nearby town of Hantsport, which enticed the American-owned Canadian Gypsum Company to build its storage and shipping facility where it got the best tax rate.

As in other small communities, religion played an important, stabilizing role in the Windsor area. When the first post-Deportation immigrants arrived, they built a simple chapel school that served people of all faiths, as a place for school on weekdays and for worship on Sundays. In effect, there was "church union" in the town at that time. In 1772 James Murdoch, an Irish-born, Scottish-educated missionary of the Church of Scotland arrived, and first lived at Horton and then at Ardoise. He travelled central Nova Scotia on horseback, preaching in homes

VIEW FROM CHAPEL HILL AFTER THE GREAT FIRE, 1897

to small Presbyterian congregations. Many of the Loyalists who came to Nova Scotia following the American Revolution were Baptist, and established a Baptist community at Windsor with a building in 1820.

There were also Methodist, Anglican, Presbyterian, and Catholic congregations in Windsor. In 1925 there was a move across Canada to unite protestant churches. In Windsor, some people decided it was a good idea but more decided otherwise. The Baptists were invited by others to unite, but were not interested. As a result, the Presbyterians joined the Methodists—but continued to use the same buildings as before, with no actual union of services taking place. Those Presbyterians who did not favour union decided to build a new, smaller church on the other end of King Street, far removed from the parent church. That church still exists with a small congregation. Instead of two churches becoming one, as intended, the result was three church buildings. Eventually, in 1967, Trinity United (formerly Methodist) and Saint John's United (formerly Presbyterian) began holding services together, in one building one week and the other building the next. By 1976, they had sold the smaller (Trinity) building and constructed a Sunday school in the previously unfinished basement of the larger church.

In 1897, at the peak of the town's glory, four-fifths of its buildings were destroyed by the so-called "Great Fire of Windsor." Fortunately, there was no loss of life in the fire, nor was the spirit of the town's people broken by their incredible losses. Windsorians quickly set about rebuilding their town, and photos from before and after the fire show their resilience and determination.

The general appearance of the town has been described in glowing terms. Indeed, many of the buildings constructed following the devastating fire of 1897 were architectural masterpieces that would serve to attract tourism to the town. Unfortunately, without forethought as to the future benefits of retaining the buildings, most were destroyed beginning in the 1950s after reaching the age of a mere fifty years and were replaced with single-storey shopping malls and other more common brick structures. Still, the ambience that the remaining Victorian buildings add to the natural beauty of this small town of beautiful rolling hills and valleys is cherished by residents and visitors alike.

Chapter 1

Transportation, the Key to Growth

ISAIAH SMITH'S COACH, C.1870

The first road in Nova Scotia that was fit for travel was between Halifax and Windsor, and was created in the early nineteenth century. By 1816, Isaiah Smith established the first stagecoach line in the Maritimes, between the two communities.

Its purpose was mainly to provide transportation to Haligonians wishing to go to Windsor, as the attraction of the small town was far greater to Haligonians than a trip to the city was to most Windsorians. Windsor's attractions were many and the town had much to offer, while the city and its many detractions was a place for most to avoid. Politicians needing to attend the legislature and students at King's Collegiate and College used the coach to travel to Halifax. The trip took six hours, the fee was six pounds, and the coach accommodated six passengers. There were several stops along the way for changes of horses and travellers, and for meals and comfort. The ultimate hope was that valley farm produce could be transported to the city regularly and in large quantities.

By 1829, the stagecoach service was extended from Halifax to Annapolis Royal, twice a week. The one remaining problem was crossing the Avon River by ferry, which could only happen twice a day, once each way, on the high tide.

WOODEN COVERED HIGHWAY BRIDGE, 1869

When this bridge was built in 1836, it was the longest covered bridge in Nova Scotia. There had long been a need for a bridge to cross the Avon River before the first was built. Originally, the only practical way of crossing the Avon River was to walk over the riverbed when the tide had receded to its lowest level. This method was used by the Mi'kmaq and Acadians, who found the shallowest part of the river on the upstream, south side of what is now Windsor. The first trail from Halifax to Windsor ran through what we now call Three Mile Plains, along the Back Road to Chester Road and then followed close to the South Mountain to the crossing. The original crossing was too far upriver from the town to be of practical use once the town developed, however, and a new fording site was established. It was still a great inconvenience to cross in that manner, and occasionally an animal had to be roped and pulled to safety by a team of oxen or horses. Some would drown, stuck in the mud.

By 1802, a covered bridge had been built between Windsor Forks and Upper Falmouth, and then in 1836 this bridge was built. The toll house can be seen on the left near the entrance to the bridge. Minimal fees were charged for horses and passengers and a locked gate prevented passage through the dark of night as there was no street lighting then. A sign at the entrance instructed people to walk their horses, so as not to jar the bridge from its moorings over time. The five-span wooden structure was thirty-three years old when this photo was taken, and it can be seen to be sagging under the stresses of years of crossings by horses and wagons. The wooden rail fence at roadside on the approach to the bridge was also in disrepair and tilting toward the riverbed, shown at low tide.

By the time the bridge began to sag at the joints, raising fears of its collapse, it had served farmers, tradespeople, and travellers for fifty-one years. It was replaced with an iron structure in 1887. On the evening following the opening celebrations, the old wooden bridge mysteriously caught fire and fell into the river in gigantic sections. A wind was blowing and pushed the flaming pieces toward the Windsor shoreline, requiring men to use long poles to push them back into the outgoing stream toward Minas Basin to prevent the town from burning. Windsor residents blamed Falmouth boys for starting the fireworks, while Falmouth people naturally blamed the Windsor youth for the flaming celebration!

Along by the Avon (Kissing Bridge) Windsor, N.S.

NEW KISSING BRIDGE, 1869

Many old covered bridges in North America are called "kissing bridges." The name indicates a hidden place for lovers to kiss, undetected. However, the kissing bridge in Windsor, built as early as 1869, was a walking bridge, built on a trestle high above the railway tracks. The name came to be because the two ends of the bridge "kissed" the adjoining embankments on either side of the railway cut to the river's edge. Then again, perhaps the folks in Windsor didn't mind kissing in public, as it were, not confining their romantic expressions to hidden places!

In this early photo of the Kissing Bridge, a lone man is seen walking from the river road toward Ferry Hill on his way to Water Street and town. Because the bridge was wooden, it required annual repairs. When automobiles became commonplace in the early 1920s, the bridge had to be replaced with a narrower one so as to discourage anybody from driving a vehicle across it—it would be unsafe for such an adventure.

People who grew up in Windsor when the Avon River was still intact have memories of a truly unique experience. The tide came and went twice a day, allowing ships to come and go while the water was there, but ships could also stay over for a day or two for the completion of a large loading task if need be. The reason had to do with the natural shape of the river bottom on the Windsor side of the river. The centre of the riverbed was a very deep channel, allowing for tides as high as sixty feet to occur without washing ashore. While the shoreline on the Falmouth, or west, side of the river falls rather sharply down, the shoreline on the Windsor, or east, side slopes gradually down to the channel. That allowed for wharves to be built to accommodate ships coming in on the tide, tying up to the wharf, and resting on the slope when the tide was out. The deck remained at wharf level. This explains why the Windsor side of the river developed into the shipping town of Windsor and the Falmouth side remained an agricultural area. Prior to the age of steam, the schooners and brigs used for shipping were all approximately the same size, and wharves were built to accommodate them as shown. The visiting wooden ship, *J. Scott Hankinson* of Weymouth, was but one of the many ships that came from ports all over the world. Next, larger wharves were built a little further down the slope, accommodating the larger and taller iron ships.

SCHOONER AND TUG, 1890s

The advent of steam-powered boats changed shipping patterns on the Avon River and Bay of Fundy. Large schooners could be guided, safely and quickly, against rough tidal waters by small but powerful tugboats to the Bay of Fundy. There, sails would take over for the journey to US ports. Before long, large cargo ships were constructed, dwarfing the loads formerly carried by schooners. There was a transition period while a fleet of iron ships was being assembled by world shipyards, during which schooners were converted to barges and used to carry gypsum. Since the tugboats that pulled the new barges were responsible for navigation as well as power, the schooner-barges no longer required full crews of sailors. Therefore a mere skeleton crew, often a husband and wife and sometimes their small family, was retained on each barge. The barges then continued to be used for transporting pulp wood, pit props for use in mines, and lumber until their days of usefulness had ended. Eventually, they were left on riverbanks to rot and sink into the mud flats.

M. V. Avon, A Ferry Boat, c.1900

From the earliest crossings of the Avon River at low tide by people and animals on foot, folks were looking for a better way to bridge the gap between the east and west banks. Eventually small rowboats were used to ferry people across. Next came barges pulled by rowboats, for animals. In 1836, a four-span covered bridge was built—the longest one ever constructed in Nova Scotia. This solved the problem for those who lived by the bridges.

But people up and down the river also needed to get across the river. The first schooner known to accommodate passengers was the *T. B. Smith*, also known as the Summerville Packet. Next was the *Maggie Van*, built in 1865 for Richard Musgrave. In 1880, the Churchill shipyard in Hantsport built the *Pinafore*, a fifteen-ton steamship that travelled between Hobart's Wharf at Summerville and Windsor, transporting people and goods from place to place along the Avon River shores.

The *Pinafore* was replaced with the *M. V. Avon*, also built by the Churchill Yard. It was said to have a narrow bow, a round bottom, little cargo space, and to be top heavy. It served for twenty-two years and when it was becoming waterlogged and unfit for transporting people, it was taken to Halifax Harbour, where it was used to transport freshwater to ships in the harbour. It spent its last days beached and rotting at the shore of Bedford Basin, where it could be seen by passing motorists for several years.

This is the iron railway bridge built in 1869 to accommodate the new Windsor and Annapolis Railway crossing, next to the 1887 pedestrian and wagon bridge. In 1857, the first section of the proposed Nova Scotia Railway between Halifax and Windsor was completed. One person, one horse, and one wagon (not to exceed six hundred pounds) would be carried from Mount Uniacke to Halifax for fifty cents on railway flatcars. Thus the railway went into business in Nova Scotia. "As many as fourteen cars of wagons have been conveyed at one time to Halifax," according to the announcement in the newspaper a short time later.

At the same time, the remainder of the railway line between Mount Uniacke and Windsor was under construction. The first trip of a single engine and one flatcar was made all the way from the city to Windsor on December 30, 1857.

On Thursday, June 3, 1858, the first train for public use arrived in Windsor at eleven in the morning packed to the gunnels with people. So exciting was the event that the whole town turned out at the new station to meet the "first train" of the new Nova Scotia Railway. A regular schedule went into effect immediately, with a train to and from Windsor each day. Because two trains operated at the same time—between eight and eleven each morning and half past two and six each afternoon, daily—they had to pass on a side-rail at Mount Uniacke. Travellers could spend three hours at their destination before boarding the train for a return trip. The one-way fare was $1.35 first class and $.87 second class.

Avon Bridges and "Flying Bluenose," Windsor, N.S.

THE FLYING BLUENOSE, 1910

The engines of the Dominion Atlantic Railway all had shiny brass nameplates. Names such as Champlain, Poutrincourt, DeMonts, Pontgrave, Lescarbot, DeRazilly, Membertou, Cornwallis, Blomidon, Haliburton, and Joe Howe echoed the history of Nova Scotia, particularly the land of Acadia. Perhaps most famous of all was the Flying Bluenose, which carried mail, freight and passengers from Halifax to Yarmouth on a daily run in the first half of the twentieth century. It is shown here arriving at Windsor in 1910 on its return route from Yarmouth, exiting from the Basket Bridge over the Avon River and about to pass beneath the Kissing Bridge. From there, it went right through the centre of town to the DAR station, blowing its whistle at all six street crossings and bringing highway traffic to a standstill.

GYPSUM TRAIN AND CABOOSE, 1910

The shadows indicate it was sunny and late afternoon as DAR Engine No. 27 arrived with a string of old-fashioned gypsum rail carts from the western area of the county for delivery to the waterfront.

This photo was taken at the corner of King and Water streets long before Water Street was paved. Lumber is piled to the left of the train engine in readiness for construction of the Windsor Tribune Building, completed in 1914. The Victoria Hotel and the Wilcox, Curry, Blanchard, and Lynch Buildings can all be seen in the background.

Gypsum was regularly loaded onto schooners at Windsor's wharves and shipped to New England. The carts were low, box-type affairs, the side panel of which would open when the box was tipped sideways. That allowed the gypsum to slide onto a chute directed to the ship's hold. Train tracks were built along the edge of the government wharf to accommodate both the schooners and the railway and longshore crews.

HORSE AND BUGGY, C.1900

MCLAUGHLIN BUICK, C.1910

People who owned hotels often owned beautiful horse-drawn carriages as well. This photo shows the owner of the Victoria Hotel, John Doran, in the early 1900s with his wife, Molly, and two children, Owen and Kathleen, driving through the countryside with a pair of horses and a fine double-seated carriage. The canopy at the back could be elevated easily in case of rain.

By 1910, a new made-in-Canada automobile named the McLaughlin Buick appeared in Windsor. The body was made in Ontario by the McLaughlin firm, which had previously specialized in making beautiful horse-drawn carriages. They now added American-made Buick motors to them to produce a motorized carriage—the McLaughlin Buick, shown here with part of the Doran family aboard for a new kind of drive through the country.

CLARKE– McGEACHY WHARF, C.1910

The gypsum trade with the US began in Windsor as early as 1760, but the Clarke–McGeachy Wharf, built in 1800, was Windsor's first significant wharf. It was located opposite the end of Albert Street, and was built by John Clarke and Neil McGeachy for the specific purpose of shipping gypsum to New England. Gypsum was Windsor's first export and remains the chief export from the area to this day. It was first controlled by local entrepreneurs but it is now American controlled. Thomas Chandler Haliburton acquired the wharf and other land from Clarke in 1830 and entered the gypsum-quarrying business. He added six gypsum-storage buildings to the wharf site, and also built a trolley track for horse-drawn carts on a corduroy road from the large quarries on his own property on Park Street (now Clifton Avenue) to the river. He thus established the business of regular shipping on the Avon.

This 1910s photo shows an advanced and speedier state of loading sailing ships with gypsum, one hundred years after Haliburton's workers did the same job with shovels, moving gypsum from horse-drawn carts to ships. Fifty years later the system became mechanized, and, as now, machinery and conveyor belts moved the gypsum.

S.S. Rotundus on the Avon River, Windsor, N.S.

S. S. ROTUNDUS, 1910

In 1910, a group of men in charge of the Avon River ferry service bought a new ship, built at the McKay shipyard of Shelburne. Shareholders paid $5,000 for a ship they named *Rotundus* because it was to make daily round trips on the Avon River. The *Rotundus* provided a valuable service for twenty-seven years to those who lived down the shore, or north of town. (Those who lived up the shore could easily access Windsor for supplies by road.) Those living in the small hamlets strung out down shore from Windsor were separated from the town by the Saint Croix River, which was never bridged at the level of the town. It meant a trip of ten to thirty miles by horse and wagon around the shores of the Saint Croix for those people to reach Windsor. Over the years, the ferry boats *Pinafore*, *Avon* and *Rotundus* allowed them to go to town, do their shopping, and return on the same tide, all within a couple of hours.

The top photo shows the Rotundus on its first trip, leaving the dock at Summerville in the spring of 1910 with a full load of excited passengers on board. A round-trip ticket cost fifty cents for all over the age of twelve, while children travelled free of charge. Captain Terfry, Mate Fred Marsters and Engineer Colin "Colie" Munroe were the permanent crew. The *Rotundus* served folks in the rural communities along the shores of the Avon River for twenty-seven years, but it rested at the dock in Summerville all winter. That meant that folks along the shore had no means of shopping from December until April and therefore had to have supplies in their homes to last for four months.

The *Rotundus* worked until 1937 and was the last ferry boat to be used on the Avon River, for by then, cars, trucks, and buses had taken over the service to those communities. The *Rotundus* followed the S. S. *Avon* to Halifax Harbour to be used as a work boat.

SMITH'S COAL WHARF AND STORAGE SHEDS, 1918

Tall ships from Glace Bay and Sydney, Cape Breton, unloaded coal and coke at high tide at Smith's and Dimock's wharves. Bennett Smith was Windsor's great shipbuilder in the mid to late 1800s, and his son Harris S. Smith had a coal and coke business on Water Street, close to the Avon River. Smith's Wharf, situated at the back of the storage sheds and Water Street business office, made for easy access to new shipments. It was a busy and lucrative venture in the era before oil was used for heating fuel. The difficulty was the amount of handling that was required to get the coal from mine to household. The underground mining process, with intensive work, holds constant danger of cave-in or explosion. Once the coal arrived at the surface, it then had to be shovelled by hand from horse-drawn dump carts to ships' storage holds at dockside. The reverse process occurred at places like Smith's Wharf. From the ship's hold, the coal was taken by dump cart, once again, to the storage sheds on the Smith property. From there it was shovelled back onto dump carts and delivered to the backyards of customers about the town. In turn, they had to shovel it into a coal room in their basements through windows especially made in the basement wall for that purpose. Most houses had matching basement windows in the driveway that led to twin coal- and wood-storage rooms.

WINTER ON THE AVON RIVER, c.1920

In the 1920s and 1930s, Bob Redden's Wharf was a real curiosity to locals and visitors alike. It was the site of Windsor's first wharf, the Clarke–McGeachy wharf of 1800, and it was Bob Redden's home and place of business; he made a living doing carpentry and building small boats in his workshop on the wharf. When the tide was right, he was also a fisherman who sold fish caught in the Avon River and Minas Basin. Bob got his drinking water from a natural spring across from his home at the foot of Ferry Hill. Because his house was on the wharf overlying the river and not on Windsor land, he paid no town taxes!

The ice cakes shown here formed as far away as the Bay of Fundy and its several tributaries. As the tide came and went, the cakes flowed in and out until they became so numerous that they jammed together and floated on the surface, completely covering the river like frosting on a cake. The tide flowed out beneath them, leaving them stranded on the riverbed. The incoming tide raised them up again, and again, twice each day. They steadily got bigger as the winter wore on, and finally clogged the riverbed completely, making shipping impossible in winter months. The large cakes bumped into the bridges and wharves as they shunted back and forth. At the height of the process, bitter cold air blew in across the ice flow and over the town from the north, making for very cold winters. Then, as spring approached, the process gradually reversed. The ice cakes got smaller and finally disappeared so that the beautiful tidal bore could be seen once again.

Canada's First Railway Gates, c.1920

The protective railway gates of Windsor were Canada's first. Built in 1869 as the Nova Scotia Railway was extended from Windsor to the Annapolis Valley, they served to block sidewalk and highway traffic while trains passed through the middle of town. Controlled by the use of a metal crank, the operation fell to physically impaired men who would otherwise have had difficulty finding work. Gate keeper Perry Lake, who had one leg amputated, is seen here to the far left with his back to the camera, watching a Dominion Day parade on the still-unpaved Gerrish Street. A right-arm amputee named Maurice "Pie" Holden also worked the gates during the early decades of the 1900s. After World War Two, a returning veteran soldier and left-arm amputee named Hughie Lyghtle took over the position until the Causeway was constructed in 1970 and the railway route was changed to cross the river directly, without traversing streets and sidewalks.

PETER MACKINNON'S CAR, 1920S

Getting a first car back in the 1920s and 1930s was about as exciting as life got. This 1919 Ford belonged to Peter MacKinnon and was named "I'm Alone," after a rum-runner on the South Shore of Nova Scotia that Pete and his young friends had heard of. Pete had mechanical aptitude from early youth and eventually became a master automobile mechanic, owning his own garage and service station on Water Street. He worked long hours in his garage, but allowed several of his friends the pleasure of driving around in the car during the day, provided they put in the necessary gas and oil! One of Pete's close friends, Frank Fox, is shown here in control of the car, with his dog Spark along for the ride.

SEAPLANE ON THE AVON RIVER, 1925

Airplanes were an incredibly uncommon sight in Windsor even in the 1930s, which explains why so many people turned out on the government wharf to view this early-model double-wing Curtis seaplane, with wing-tip-pontoons, that landed on the Avon River close to high tide. The plane was transporting an official Canadian Government Photographic Team doing the first aerial photography of the province. The crew came into Windsor to re-fuel, according to a *Hants Journal* report.

WINDSOR'S FIRST SCHOOL BUS, 1947

This photograph was taken at Bruce O'Brien's service station by Stephens and Yeatons Garage, Albert Street.

The Fargo panel truck on the right was purchased for $850 and was being used by Fred Boyd to transport eleven children on two wooden benches from Falmouth to Windsor Academy through the World War Two years. When Department of Education officials found out about it, they sent Murray Campbell, a school inspector, to tell Boyd that it would no longer be legal. Boyd explained that it was only a temporary arrangement, as the children had no other means of travel. He and his sons Grant and Fred Jr. then bought a second-hand 1947 Chevrolet truck for $695 and prepared to build a school bus. First they stripped it down to engine, wheels, and frame. A local welder, Grant Fowler, extended the length of the metal frame. With the help of a couple of carpenters, Walter Salter and Ernie Lawrence, they built a body for it with a painted, canvas-covered top. The local blacksmith, Claude Smith, made an iron closure apparatus for the door. The hardware dealer, John Wilcox, cut plate glass for the windows. Mr. Fred Manning, owner of Pender's Bus Ltd. in Halifax and a Falmouth native, kindly supplied the second-hand seats, two wooden benches, for the students free of charge. Thus a conventional work truck became Windsor's first school bus. It travelled the rural routes picking up children and delivering them to school in good weather and foul. It travelled during storms—even if children had to get out and push at times to get it through snow or mud! On days when there was a good movie showing at the Imperial Theatre, the Boyd boys would wait an extra half hour before heading for the country to be sure that everybody saw the movie and got home safely by five o'clock in time to do the farm chores. Occasionally, when an adult required a drive to or from town for a doctor's appointment or such and had no other means of transportation, the Boyd boys obliged.

It is not known for certain if this was the first school bus in Nova Scotia, but according to students who travelled on it, it was certainly the best, and it provided them with some of the happiest days of their lives.

L–r: Fred Boyd and his dog Spot, sons Fred Jr. and Grant, employees Howard Barker and Chesley MacDonald, with the Boyd's fleet of trucks in 1947.

**S. S. Trident
Loading Lumber,
1950s**

At low tide, the government wharf stood forty feet above the wooden cradle
that ships rested on at dockside. When a ship was being loaded during low
tide, a fall of thirty feet between the wharf and ship would mean certain death,
for the cradle was made of large hardwood timbers. Parents were forever
reminding their children to stay away from there for safety's sake. Neverthe-
less, children were inquisitive and just had to look down to see for themselves
how far the ship's bottom was from the top of the wharf, or how deep the
water was. This photo taken in the 1950s shows all the wharf-side dangers
that terrified parents. While longshoremen are busy moving loads of lumber to
their partners waiting at the bottom of the ship's holds, a youth is kneeling at
wharf's edge and assessing the wharf-side situation.

Ships like this one were equipped with steam-powered winches and large
booms that allowed them to load without a crane on the wharf. Export of
lumber was still a major business from Windsor into the 1960s. Medium-sized
ships could rest on the wood cradle at river bottom with the tide out. Later,
when larger ships were built to transport gypsum, they required the pressure of
water to keep them stable and would break into pieces without it. Therefore,
when larger ships became common, they had to be loaded and leave town on
the same tide. Since Windsor was not equipped to load gypsum, transport was
impossible from the Windsor wharves. Business declined as the large ships
went to ports without tidal water.

Chapter 2

Military Life

ILLUSTRATION OF PIZIGUIT BY JOHN HAMILTON, 1753

The title of this painting reads, "View of Fort Edward in Piziguit River, Nova Scotia, painted in the year 1753 by Cap. John Hamilton of his Majesty's 40th Regiment." The blockhouse and living quarters were built by the British in 1750 high on the hill overlooking the junction of the Avon and Saint Croix rivers, with the so-called "Bird's Head" on Nesbitt's Island, distinctly marking the site.

The fort was initially built to protect the English from raids by the Mi'kmaq and Acadians. The English and French had been warring over possession of Nova Scotia for years, and the English had taken over for the last time in 1710, and founded Halifax in 1749. They then established Fort Edward and built a blockhouse and military barracks in 1750 to protect their interests from invasion by French, Mi'kmaq, or Americans through a rear corridor via Minas Basin. The fort became the gathering ground for a thousand Acadians of the Piziquid area prior to the Deportation in 1755. A military presence on the fort was maintained for many years, including the Scottish Highland Emigrants of the 84th Battalion of Foot, many of whom remained as settlers.

MILITIA AND RECRUITS AT BLOCKHOUSE ON FORT EDWARD, CANADA'S OLDEST REMAINING MILITARY STRUCTURE, 1896

Eventually, the fort was staffed only by militia, as seen here in 1896. The photo appears to show three young civilians with their new uniforms in hand, as they have joined the unit, members of which are lined up behind them. The three children leaning against the blockhouse show that the fort was no longer very seriously guarded by then. The officers' quarters shown in the background were destroyed by fire in 1923.

BOY BUGLERS OF NOVA SCOTIA'S 112TH BATTALION

The urge to join the army and fight for freedom, Canada's people, and England was overwhelming for many Canadian youth when the Great War broke out in 1914. Many of those of age immediately signed up as soldiers. Younger boys longed to become sixteen and join the others. Windsor youth, just like youngsters across the nation, would lie about their age to recruiting offices and were often accepted into the army. Up until 1915, Jimmy Vaughan (centre, middle row) and two good friends, Fred Mounce (second from left, middle row) and Johnny Hughes (centre, front row), had only ever worn short pants in summer, and knee-length jodhpur trousers with knee stockings in cooler months—boys' clothes at the time. In an effort to appear older, they gathered the necessary dollars and went to Frank Roach's clothing store on Gerrish Street to buy their first pairs of long pants. They next appeared at the recruiting office at Fort Edward looking quite mature, so they thought, and told the necessary lie, "We are sixteen years old!" However, they didn't keep their long pants for long—they became soldiers all right, with full uniforms: cap, badges, and khaki jodhpurs! They no longer wore stockings, but puttees—rolls of three-inch khaki cloth that soldiers wrapped around the tops of their boots and lower legs to the snug part of the jodhpurs at the knee, as displayed by the boys in the photo. The youth became "boy buglers" in the military band of the 112th battalion, and were billeted in pup tents on Fort Edward for preliminary training. Before long they were shipped overseas to Aldershot Camp in England for further training. By the time another year passed and they were truly sixteen years of age, they found themselves in the thick of battle at Passchendaele, Ypres, and Vimy Ridge. Luckily, these three survived and returned home after the 1918 victory and became members of the Great War Veterans Association and of the British Empire Service League.

Fort Edward was a training ground for battalions from across Canada and other parts of the Commonwealth in World War One. A British expeditionary detachment was stationed at the fort for a time in 1918. This unlikely pair of friends was often seen together about town. Corporal Williams was from London, England, and at thirty-nine years old he was six feet, seven inches tall, and weighed 260 pounds. Private Henri was from Paris, France, and was known as the "Tom Thumb" of the detachment. He was thirty years old, just under five feet tall, and weighed 122 pounds. Very affable types, they usually appeared together, to the pleasure and amusement of people wherever they turned up. This photo was taken in January 1918 on Gerrish Street in front of the *Hants Journal* office.

JEWISH LEGION AT FORT EDWARD, 1918

Jewish citizens of the United States who were sympathetic to the Allied cause formed their own battalion, and came to Windsor in 1918 for final training before going to fight in Europe. Of note is the fact that David Ben-Gurion was one of the soldiers. He later became the first prime minister of Israel. The troops are shown here billeted on the slope of Fort Edward with the old blockhouse and officers' quarters at the top of the hill.

TENTS ON FORT EDWARD, 1916

The 85th and 112th Battalions, made up of young men from the region, were billeted in tents on the grounds of Fort Edward as they underwent military training prior to going overseas in the Great War, which began in 1914. Battalions came from elsewhere in Canada for a time as well. The surface of the hill was covered with canvas tents to house these men, who were always coming and going. This photo shows a section of the tents as well as church steeples and smoke stacks of the town towering in the background.

RETURNING GREAT WAR VETERANS, 1918

A group of returning war veterans are greeted by a crowd of citizens at the Windsor railway station following the Great War of 1914-18. Percy Kilcup of the 85th Battalion is at the head of the group. He wears a wedge cap with 85th Battalion metal insignia on it. A crutch handle can be seen beneath his left arm. Notice that all eyes are directed toward Percy in his great moment of glory as a local war hero.

Thirty-five Windsor men died overseas during World War One. Those who returned filled a variety of jobs and learned new trades. Amputees, who faced particular employment challenges, often found work as nightwatchmen, time-keepers on construction sites, and janitors in factories.

PERCY KILCUP, 1918

Percy Kilcup was a dispatch rider, on bicycle, wounded in France. His injuries necessitated the amputation of his left leg. He wore an artificial limb and worked the rest of his life at a variety of jobs to support his wife and a family of three.

WINDSOR ACADEMY CADET BAND, 1918

The Windsor Academy Haig Cadet Corps was formed following the Boer War and honoured General Douglas Haig, who in World War One led Canadian troops in Europe, including Windsor's soldiers in battles in France.

The Bugle Band of the cadet corps was popular with students and town citizens alike. In fact, during World War One the band was in demand for parades for several battalions billeted at Fort Edward, for some such battalions did not have their own military band.

The Bugle Band was the beginning of a career in music for some. H. Carleton Smith and his brother Sid, shown in this photo, got their start there and played in the Windsor Citizens' Band into their senior years.

Back Row (l–r): Halley Jenkins, Lawrence Roach, Cliff Shaw, Gordon "Doggie" Kuhn, Gordon Vaughan, Peter Jadis; centre row: Bliss DeMont, George Hughes, Carleton Smith, Ernie Mosher, Ralph Sweet; front row: Lloyd Taylor, Sidney Smith.

HAIG CADET CORPS ARMISTICE DAY SALUTE, 1923

At eleven o'clock on the morning of November 11, 1923, the Windsor Academy Haig Cadet Corps was in formation at the dedicated cenotaph. With the flag lowered, a two minute silence is being observed. The young cadets are showing respect for fallen soldiers as they learn to be soldiers themselves. Many children and parents wearing winter clothing on the cold, bright morning are lined up at the edge of Victoria Park, taking part in the Armistice Day Ceremony.

Made of Quebec granite, the cenotaph represents a Celtic cross, embedded sword of sacrifice, dove of peace, and two hemispheres. Here, it lists the names of those who died in the Great War. (In 1995, names of those who served in World War Two and the Korean War were added to granite blocks and placed beneath the hemispheres.) Ever since the first dedication in 1923, the Remembrance Day ceremony has been held at the cenotaph.

"WEST NOVIES" IN ENGLAND, 1940

With the onset of World War Two, Windsor youth signed up for military service. Within the year, many of them had completed training in Canada and were overseas in England for advanced training before shipping off to the European War Fronts. These members of the West Nova Scotia Regiment were doing Bren Gun Carrier training in England when this photo was taken in 1940. Billy Graham, left, and Ted Kilcup (son of Percy) are standing with their Sergeant. Soon after this was taken, the soldiers were in the Battle of Ortona, Italy, where Ted was killed in action.

Careless Talk Costs Lives, 1943

In this photo, Mayor Ira B. Lohnes poses with the camp commandant and four soldiers displaying a sign that appeared on Wentworth Road from 1943 to 1945. It was the idea and creation of the four soldiers who, in peacetime, were in the business of advertising and illustration.

The sign was a reminder to Windsorians to avoid talking to others about what was happening in their town.

Photos taken during World War Two at the Acadia Barracks of No. 1 Army Transit Camp, in Windsor, are few and far between. It was a top-secret wartime operation, not to be photographed, visited, or publicized. Thousands of military personnel came by train directly into the camp's railway yard in the night, and disappeared just as silently days or weeks later. They headed by train to ships at Halifax, then waited at anchor in Bedford basin until they sailed in convoys for Britain.

The No. 1 Army Transit Camp was the third largest Military Camp in Canada with a staff of five hundred and a modern, 275-bed hospital ready to tend to war casualties, if necessary. The camp facilities could accommodate ten thousand men and were built to be used for several years after the war was won. The one thing the camp did not have was stores for shopping of any kind. Consequently, soldiers on day-leave frequently cleaned out Windsor's stores and restaurants of supplies. On one occasion, just prior to a huge shipment of troops out of the camp, supplies in town were lowered so drastically that some stores and restaurants had to close temporarily because of lack of food and supplies. The fact that so many purchases were made was the only signal people had of the gigantic troop movement, as all lips were sealed—after all, "Careless Talk Costs Lives."

While in Windsor, in order to keep in shape, the battalions of men performed daily route marches through the streets of town in full battle dress, with backpacks and rifles. They filled the streets as far as one could see, forward and back. Leading them were some of the greatest military bands a Windsorian could ever expect to see or hear. Imagine for instance, a Scottish pipe band in tartans with Highland kilts and sporrans, six men abreast, using kettle drums, side drums, and double bass drums, all led by a magnificently dressed drum major wearing a beaver hat, white leather cuffs, and spats, who threw his gloriously carved baton into the air and caught it flawlessly each time as it returned to his well-trained fist. Drill sergeant majors called out commands as necessary. All eyes were straight ahead, arms swinging shoulder high with amazing precision. Every soldier was in step with the loud drum beat, and the thunderous stomp of their boots in unison was both scary and inspiring for people now afraid of the effects of war. Even without the fire of a single rifle, the troops were a commanding and frightening site to behold. They were not all Canadians. There were platoons of allies from Australia, New Zealand, South Africa, the United States, and other United Nations countries, notable by the variation of their outfits, though they were obviously united by purpose. Townsfolk observed in quiet amazement. The streets of Windsor have never seen such action and felt such excitement before or since.

There was romance associated with the army camp as well. Wives and sweethearts of soldiers temporarily stationed here were allowed to visit for a few days. They came by train or bus from various parts of the country and found room and board with families around town who could spare a bed and wanted to assist. It wasn't that locals could realize any great profit from providing the service, as room and board was then a mere $7 a week. It did allow couples to meet for a few days before the soldier went overseas. For some, it was their last visit.

Following World War Two, the camp was converted to a rehabilitation centre for veterans. They were trained in various trades before re-entering the workforce. The buildings were eventually dismantled and the wood and equipment were sold as surplus to be used in building new homes in Windsor and area.

Chapter 3

The Fire Department and the Great Fire

WORLD CHAMPION HOSE REEL TEAM, 1888

Veni, Vidi, Vinci (I came, I saw, I conquered) is the slogan the Windsor firefighters used to welcome back their winning team from a competition in Halifax in 1886. The team had just become World Champion Hose Runners in a provincial tournament in Halifax. The Windsor fire department was made up of volunteers, and entering competitions such as this helped them to hone their skills. This photo shows the winning team with a hose reel and the valuable Silver Trumpet Trophy they won along with $300 as they set a new world record for the half-mile hose reel race in a Nova Scotia Firefighters Tournament. Unfortunately, even these champions couldn't save the town from a vicious fire a decade later.

THE MARINE BLOCK AND SAIL LOFT, 1896

On October 17, 1897, Windsor suffered a devastating fire that would entirely change the face of the downtown core. This is the site at which the Great Fire began. Windsor was a very busy shipping centre at the time with an extensive wharf system and many schooners coming and going and requiring maintenance. Ships and their sails were repaired here at the marine block. Oil, tar, canvas, rope, and dry wood were stored in buildings covered with wooden shingles—all very combustible materials. Newspaper accounts of the fire reported a small fire having begun on the evening of October 17 and being extinguished by the town's bucket brigade. But well after midnight, when most of the town's people were asleep, a strong wind began to blow in from Minas Basin and the Bay of Fundy. The fire, fanned by the wind, broke out again and quickly spread to adjacent buildings and grew out of control.

VIEW OF GERRISH STREET, OCTOBER 18, 1897

This is probably the most dramatic photograph taken by local photographer Wesley Livingston on the morning following the destruction of Windsor by fire. These people had just lost all of their belongings, and had escaped with only the clothing on their bodies. Silhouetted against the early morning sun, they are milling about at one of the town's busiest areas, the junction of Water and Gerrish streets, where the railway tracks crossed the centre of the Windsor's commercial and traffic areas. The glorious stone structure on the right was the Gibson Hotel building, with old-fashioned English chimney pots and thick field-stone walls. To the left is the beautifully designed federal post office building (1884). Beyond are the remains of the courthouse, jail, and the chimneys of homes.

**PEGGY LEITCH
AFTER THE GREAT
FIRE, OCTOBER 18,
1897**

Peggy Leitch was ninety-one years old when she was photographed surveying the damage to the town on the morning after the Great Fire. The remains of a small Acorn-brand stove, made at the Windsor Foundry, is seen in the charred rubble to her immediate right. Leitch is obviously awestricken, disbelieving of the massive destruction. She must have felt truly alone, as she had no living relatives and possessed very little material wealth. She was indeed a poor woman, who had long lived with the family of Bennett Smith, Windsor's great shipbuilder. They had taken her in from the poor house to be a nursemaid for their young children many years before. Following the fire, in which the Smith home and belongings were burned, a new house was built and Leitch, fortunately, remained with the family, cared for as ever. When the Smiths finally died, their daughter Elizabeth kept Leitch in her home until Leitch died in 1901 at age ninety-five. She was buried in the Smith family plot at Maplewood Cemetery.

When the losses were tallied following the Great Fire of 1897, it was estimated that four-fifths of the town's buildings had burned. The wind, coming in off of the river, blew cinders from west to east and not in a north–south direction, and homes on Nesbitt Street to the north and Ferry Hill to the south were spared. In the centre of this photo is a three-storey house at the corner of Avon and Elm streets. Beyond it are homes on Chestnut Street belonging to the Wilcox and Shand families and others. The foreground shows rubble and basements extending from Gerrish Street across Stannus and Albert streets to the foot of Ferry Hill.

**RELIEF TICKETS
TENT ON
BURNHAM'S HILL,
1897**

This military guard was part of a contingent from Halifax to help prevent pilferage and vandalism following the Great Fire. He's standing guard while a volunteer hands out relief tickets for food and other necessities from a makeshift counter in a military tent. The site is on the side of Burnham's Hill just next to the parking lot of the DAR Station.

A man with the last name Fletcher, left, was immediately accused of starting the Great Fire, but his involvement was never proven, and the accusation itself seems to have been the product of racism in Windsor. Fletcher was the only independent black businessman in the town; he owned a small restaurant on the Marine Wharf, where he served alcoholic drinks to some patrons. He was involved with a few confrontations with the town Temperance Society, which had been pressuring him to stop serving alcohol—during the late nineteenth century, many hotels and restaurants faced similar situations.

Fletcher is here being interviewed by a reporter from the *Halifax Herald* the day after the fire.

First Post–
Great Fire Home,
1897

Frederick Lavers and his family lived on Grey Street and lost their home in the fire. All they managed to save was a carpenter's tool chest, seven chairs, an apple basket, a fishing creel, and two framed pictures. Lavers gathered pieces of fence boards from the neighbourhood and built a small shack for his family. With this construction, thus began the rebuilding of the town, in a very unique place and way!

Lavers chose to build his eight-by-ten foot fence-board shack at the east end of a tunnel joining the east and west quarries on Thomas Chandler Haliburton's old property, as the east quarry was no longer in use at the time of the fire. As Lavers gathered a few windows and a door in days following, he refined the living quarters, which lasted until better accommodation could be arranged.

The Steam
Pumper, 1900

Bill Sloan, shown standing by the pumper, was the volunteer in charge of the glorious brass Ronald-brand steam pumper newly acquired by the Volunteer Fire Department following the devastating fire of 1897. He worked as a steam locomotive engineer on the Dominion Atlantic Railway, so he was well trained for his new position with the Fire Department. The driver of the beautiful white horse team that pulled the pumper was Joe Dill. Bill, Joe, and other volunteers took their positions very seriously and also raised the funds needed to acquire modern equipment for readiness in case of fire.

THE WINDSOR VOLUNTEER FIRE DEPARTMENT, 1920

Each spring the Windsor Fire Department Volunteers feature a Fire Awareness and Cleanup Week. This 1920 photo was taken during one such event in front of the fire shed, located in the civic building on Gerrish Street. The department had just acquired its first motorized vehicle, appropriately named after the river, "Avon." Note the brass dome of the department's first steam-powered water pumper on the middle wagon, which was acquired at the same time. Nearby livery stables supplied horses that were quickly retrieved and backed into the shafts of the wagons and harness. Valuable time was frequently lost in the harnessing of the horses to equipment. The advent of motorized equipment was a great step forward in firefighting.

The firefighters atop the equipment are all dressed in rubber raincoats and hats, while the driver, W. A. "Billy" Stephens and Fire Chief George Smith display the dress uniform of the firefighters, used for marching parades and formal occasions.

KING STREET FIRE, NOVEMBER 1924

By 1924, the volunteer fire department had acquired a Ronald steamer for pumping water, as well as the Avon fire engine. However, on November 9, 1924, when a fire broke out on the waterfront, burning the H. S. Smith coal office building and spreading quickly across the street to the homes on the north side of King Street, the department found it needed still more equipment and trained men to handle such a fire. Many fine homes that had been constructed following the 1897 fire were suddenly involved in another conflagration.

Chapter 4

Churches, Schools, and Medical Care

THE WINDSOR BAPTIST CHURCH, C.1899

The Windsor Baptist Church was formed on December 4, 1819, and services were held upstairs in a house on Gerrish Street. The Lord's Supper was celebrated for the first time by the church on February 27, 1820. Also that year, the first church was built on Stannus Street, near Victoria Street.

A new house of worship was built and opened for service in the autumn of 1850, the land on King Street opposite the flatiron park having been donated by Peter Shand. Services were held every Sunday until the church was destroyed in the Great Fire. By the following week, the governors of King's College had offered the use of the Convocation Hall for church services. Fire insurance of ten thousand dollars was awarded the congregation, and the following June plans were made to build a new church on the same site at a cost of fourteen thousand dollars. The church was completed in June 1899 and seated thirteen hundred people. It was one of the finest in the Maritimes. In 1949, a fire broke out inside the Sunday school and destroyed the smaller of the two steeples, but the church was saved by the Windsor Volunteer Fire Department.

Another Baptist congregation existed close by, and received support from the Windsor Baptists. A group of black Loyalists settled in the Windsor Plains area in 1780, and were joined by others around 1812. Baptists, they soon set about having regular church meetings. By 1924 there were sixteen members of the congregation. Ministers visited from Halifax in due course and the congregation thrived. Student ministers from Acadia Divinity College began visiting in the 1880s and the congregation, by then of forty, decided it was time to build a church. This is where the Windsor Baptists helped out. In *A Brief History of the Coloured Baptists of Nova Scotia,* it is noted that "Their present pastor is hard worked; through his energy and assistance, mainly through the good friends of Windsor, and particularly so through Deacon A. P. Shand of Windsor, they have built an elegant little chapel, which will compare favourably with any in the province of similar surroundings, and in many instances excel others. The church has been favoured with sermons by some of the best men of the denomination. They have also in connection with the church a lively Sabbath School."

PRESBYTERIAN CHURCH, C.1896

James Murdoch, a Presbyterian missionary of Irish birth and educated in Scotland, came to Windsor from Scotland in 1772. He first settled in Horton, with all of central Nova Scotia as his pastoral charge. He travelled by horseback over narrow, primitive trails to spread the word of God. Soon he was given farmland at Ardoise, between Halifax and Windsor. He united the people and they made plans for a building of worship. The first Presbyterian Church in Windsor was built on Avonton Hill, above Vinegar Hill (King Street), in 1808. A larger building, Saint John's Presbyterian Church, was built on Vinegar Hill in 1856. It burned in 1897 and was immediately replaced. In 1925, congregations in Windsor followed others across Canada in an attempt to unite.

SALVATION ARMY IN WINDSOR, 1899

Captain Nellie Banks established the Salvation Army in a Grey Street building in Windsor in 1886. In 1899 a new citadel was built on Gerrish Street; the name and date were emblazoned beneath the cornice on the building. In addition to church services and humanitarian work, the Salvation Army promoted music and musicians all around the world. The music of a Salvation Army Band on a street corner in Windsor on a Sunday morning was a common, much-loved sound for many decades.

SALVATION ARMY SUNDAY SCHOOL CLASS, 1897

Teacher, wearing Salvation Army bonnet and gown: Mrs. William (Mary Ann) Nix; pupils: Maude King, Eva Fox, Minnie Kilcup, Flossie Sharpham, Laura Vaughan, Eva Redden, Jennie Galton, Clauda Nix.

THE ANGLICAN CHURCH, C.1900

The Anglican Church in Windsor began like others, with services at the ecumenical chapel-school at Curry's Corner in the old burying ground. King's College students and teachers also walked to the Saint Michael's Church (1863) at Windsor Forks, three miles along the road to Chester. A chapel was built on Gray Street in the centre of town in 1845 and was used until a more substantial church was constructed on King Street, beginning in 1882. The first Anglican Church in Windsor was built in 1882 and it still stands. Cinders landed on the roof in the early morning during the Great Fire, but they were noticed by Arthur Dill, eventually a Windsor dentist but just a youth at the time of the fire. He lived at the corner of Wentworth Street and King Street, directly across from the Anglican church. He was on the verandah roof of his family home putting buckets of water on the shingles in order to prevent them from catching fire, as others were doing all around him, when he noticed the cinders on the church. He and a neighbour, Mr. Macnamara, who was milking his cow, alerted a carpenter who was building the new Baptist manse across the street from the church. They took a bucket of milk and a ladder, climbed to the church roof, and extinguished the cinders to save the building.

CATHOLIC CHAPEL, C.1895

ST. JOHN'S CATHOLIC CHURCH, 1910

In 1826, the Catholic congregation in Windsor built a chapel on Albert Street, and the hill behind the street became known as Chapel Hill. Likewise, that section of Albert Street became known as Chapel Lane. A cemetery was created in the adjacent churchyard. The chapel was destroyed in the Great Fire, along with other buildings on Chapel Lane, although the cemetery still exists.

Almost immediately, the congregation built a beautiful stone church on King Street, with an attached residence for the priest. Over the years, many of the gravestones in the chapel cemetery have collapsed with age, while others have survived and remain as a memorial to the founding Catholics, who were buried at the old chapel site. A new cemetery was founded on Windmill Hill, accessible then from Vinegar Hill, now called King Street.

One photo shows the former chapel, while the other shows the new Saint John's Catholic Church built of stone. Beyond it can be seen the newly constructed Baptist Church, built of wood. Beyond are two other steeples. The nearest is of the Anglican Church, the more distant of the then-new Presbyterian Church.

THE METHODIST CHURCH, SEPTEMBER 14, 1939

The Methodist Congregation in Windsor originated in 1782 with the arrival of William Black, a young member of the Yorkshire Methodists, who gave a sermon at the home of Henry Scott on Wentworth Road. In 1792 they built a small church on the Michael Franklin Farm at Nesbitt's Island, and soon moved to King Street. The large and beautiful church built there burned in the Great Fire of 1897, and a new church was built in 1898. In 1925 the church became Trinity United Church, but it caught fire on the morning of September 14, 1939, and was completely destroyed. As shown here, the main body of the building was gutted and the roof collapsed as the steeple tower burst into flames. Firefighters continued applying water all day in a successful attempt to confine the inferno to the solitary building. A much smaller church was built in 1940 and later, following union of the congregation with Saint John's United Church to form the Windsor United Church, the building became the hall for the Independent Order of Odd Fellows, and subsequently the West Hants Historical Museum.

WINDSOR BAPTIST CHURCH WOMEN'S GROUP, 1940s

Called the Mothers' Circle, although all were not mothers, the Baptist women's group was formed in the 1940s, during World War Two, by Marjorie Hamilton, the minister's wife. The women met weekly and sewed, knitted, and quilted together to support the church and each other. Because of the high level of commitment of the members to the ideals of the organization, the group was highly successful and carried on for many years.

Back row, l-r: Pearl Bezanson, Mysie Reynolds, Mary Trenholm, Mary Smith, Lucy Saunders, Stella Levy, Mamie Walker, Mary Hartland, Evelyn Dimock, and Cassie Leighton; third row: Bertie Black, Nora Tibbets, Ruth Johnston, Lottie Wile, Elsie Rourke, Edna Reid, Laura Brown, Mary Smith, Gladys Shaw; second row: Laurena Slack, Edna Wilson (set back), Minnie Kilcup, Hazel Boyd, Florence Sawler, Edna Roach, Ella Levy, Alma Curry, Lillian Dimock, Nellie Harvey; front row: Frances Walker, Carrie Brown, Jean Levy, Frances Elliott, Marjorie Hamilton, Bertha Smith, Helen Parker, Dorothy "Dot" Parker, Olive "Ollie" Vaughan.

EDGEHILL SCHOOL FOR GIRLS, 1891 Henry Youle Hind was an English immigrant and a successful geologist who settled in Windsor at Curry's Corner on retirement. He was the driving force behind the organization that built Edgehill School, a private school for Anglican girls. It provided education equivalent to that now provided by grades seven to twelve in Nova Scotia's public schools. It was fashioned after the English private schools. The large and beautiful structure was built in 1891.

**THE WINDSOR
PUBLIC SCHOOL,
1896**

In 1865, a two-storey public school was built in the centre of town, as high-school teaching became adopted in the province. Public schools were built in each shiretown of the counties: Windsor for Hants County, Kentville for King's County, Truro for Colchester County, etc. They were to be called "county academies." KCA (King's County Academy) and CCA (Colchester County Academy) seemed to stick, but for whatever reason, Hants County Academy became known as Windsor Academy. It was an attractive and nicely proportioned building situated at the corner of Victoria Street and Chapel Lane, later called Albert Street. The school became so busy that in 1888, the town council seriously considered building a two-storey addition to the back of the building, nearly doubling its size. By 1896, the council had secured a government loan for $35,000 and made plans to replace the aging wooden structure with a new and larger stone-and-brick building. Then came the Great Fire of 1897. Because of its entirely wooden construction, the Hants County Academy was quickly engulfed in flame. Following the fire, a request was made to the provincial government for funds to build immediately, as the need then was far greater than before. The new structure was designed to be built mostly of stone and brick, making it far more fireproof than its predecessor.

THE WINDSOR ACADEMY, 1898

The magnificent new school was opened in November 1898. It was like a crown in the centre of town, topped with a glorious bell tower, dedicated to the first principal of Windsor Academy, John Arnold Smith, who was affectionately referred to by students as "Daddy" Smith. The huge cut-stone blocks that formed the base, along with the decorative cement scroll work that outlined each of the impressive five doorways, gave an air of elegance to the building that became an integral part of the lives of children in the following decades. However, by the 1940s, the walls on the third storey began to pull away from the floors and peripheral stairways. In 1946, the building was deemed unsafe for use. Classes were held for all grades in various other places in town while costly repairs took place. The third storey, roof, and bell tower were removed and structural alterations were made to prevent further deterioration. Classes resumed in the fall of 1949.

THE THOMAS CURREN SCHOOL, 1910

The Chapel School, a multi-denominational church built in 1771, served as a school on weekdays, and was certainly the first public school in Windsor. The Curren School was the second. Thomas Curren taught at King's Collegiate for twenty-five years from 1821 to 1846. When he retired, he opened a school in a small building next to his home on King Street, just beyond its junction with O'Brien Street. He was a splendid teacher and had many young students. The school building was then situated level with the sidewalk, as shown here. It was of fine construction, with plastered walls, and was well suited as a school.

KING'S COLLEGE, 1918

Loyalists who came to Nova Scotia following the American Revolution of 1780 were determined to build a college for the youth of the colony. Accordingly, in 1788, sixty-nine acres of prime pastoral land were purchased in Windsor from John Clarke, an Irish immigrant landowner. King's College School, the oldest residential school in Canada, was founded in 1788 by Bishop Charles Inglis. He was a Loyalist and the first bishop of Nova Scotia. For the first year, twenty students were taught in a house. For the next five years the school was situated in the home of Susannah Franklin, wife of Lieutenant Governor Michael Franklin. In 1790 the main administration building was begun, and by 1794, the school moved into a section of the newly constructed three-storey college building. In 1822, the school was separated from the college and was moved to a separate building on the lower campus, adjacent to College Street.

KING'S COLLEGE FIRE, 1920

The magnificent wooden administration building at King's College, with its huge wood pillars and individual student suites (each with its own fireplace leading to multiple shared chimneys) burned to the ground on February 8, 1920. Although the governors arranged for it to be rebuilt, and went so far as to lay the corner stone in 1923, it wasn't to be. For political reasons, the college was reconstructed forty-five miles away on the Studley campus of Dalhousie University in Halifax in 1923. That left only the preparatory school, King's Collegiate, functioning on the original campus.

Windsor had been a college town for 135 years, and the town suddenly lost that status. The effect of the loss of the college cannot be overemphasized. Windsor had been known as the cultural centre of Canada, and the economic advantage of having a large number of students in a small town has proven to be immense—witness the success of Antigonish, Wolfville, and Sackville, New Brunswick. Moving King's College to the already stable and growing economy of Halifax at the expense of Windsor, which was already staggering after losing the shipping and shipbuilding trade, was devastating.

DR. J. W. REID'S HOUSE CALL, 1890s

Before the age of motor vehicles and hospitals, Dr. James W. Reid used a team of horses for house calls to his patients, both in Windsor and the surrounding countryside. When his two sons, Jim and Ted, became old enough, they loved the opportunity to go along with their father on a house call, as well as the chance to handle the reins. Eventually they took over the job of driving their aging father on all calls. A little later still, they went off to college and became doctors as well. By then, their father was driving his own automobile and didn't require either horse or driver. By the time the boys graduated, automobiles were common and they entered practise in a modern age with a car always ready and waiting by the office door.

Payzant Memorial Hospital, Windsor, N.S.

PAYZANT MEMORIAL HOSPITAL, 1910

In the 1890s, there was only one hospital in the province, at Halifax. Dr. J. B. Black of Windsor pointed out to his fellow citizens that it would be to their benefit to have a hospital in town. A prominent Windsor grocer-cum-banker, Godfrey Payzant, donated twenty thousand dollars on condition that the town raise an equal amount to complete the job. Mary Wiggins donated a thousand dollars and began holding fundraisers, which raised five thousand more. The money was coming into the building fund regularly and on schedule when the Great Fire struck, bringing efforts to a halt. Dr. Black became mayor of the town and successfully petitioned the government for fourteen thousand dollars. The Blanchard family then donated land on Windmill Hill as a building site. By 1905, a thirteen-bed hospital was ready for occupancy.

A school of nursing was soon established at the hospital, and the first class graduated in 1909. Then a drive began to raise funds for a nurses' residence, and with the help of fundraising efforts by the British Expeditionary Force stationed at Fort Edward during World War One, the nurses' residence was built in 1914 at a cost of $1716.61. It was furnished by citizens.

A new wing was added to the hospital in 1930, which brought the bed count up to fifty. By the late 1940s, with the baby boom in full swing, the population increased, making the need for another addition to the hospital. Forty-five beds and eighteen bassinets, as well as a new X-Ray machine, were added in 1950. In 1959, a new surgical operating room was added. In the late 1960s plans began to gel to build a new modern institution. Building began in 1973 on a new twenty-two acre site off of Wentworth Road, and the Hants Community Hospital, with 120 beds, was complete and occupied in 1976, officially opened by Her Majesty, Queen Elizabeth II.

FREEMASON'S HOME AT WINDSOR, 1912

The idea of ensuring home care for elderly Nova Scotia Masons of limited means was first suggested by Abner Hart of Saint Andrew's Lodge of Halifax in 1888. It was explored for several years but did not gain the approval of enough Masons to succeed. When finally the plan was altered to include the purchase of a separate Masonic Home, with all Masons and their wives or widows being eligible, it gained unanimous approval at Grand Lodge, and got the approval of all lodges in the province. William M. Christie, a Mason and lawyer of Windsor, was named to the selection committee to find a suitable home to be used, and he suggested Windsor as a central location in the province, pointing out Fairfield Farm as a very suitable home for the purpose. Fairfield had been the residence of the Hon. Sampson Blowers, Chief Justice of the Supreme Court of Nova Scotia from 1797 to 1833. It was a ten-acre farm that had become a summer boarding house and later became a part of the estate of wealthy ship-builder Bennett Smith. The lodges raised twenty thousand dollars to establish the care facility. Fairfield Farm was purchased for four thousand dollars, and an annual head tax of fifty cents per Mason was levied for continued support. The Freemasons Home of Windsor opened on February 10, 1909, with ten couples as residents. In 1912, a south wing was erected so as to accommodate more guests, and two more wings were added in 1931 and 1951, this time of brick construction. An annual tax levied on each lodge in Nova Scotia, along with ever-increasing donations from the wills of Masons, created a substantial endowment fund for support of the home. In 1995, because the building no longer met safety standards for a seniors' residence, the occupants were moved elsewhere and it was destroyed.

January 3, 1944, was an exciting day for John and Esther Beckwith of Hantsport, as well as for the new class of young nurses at the Payzant Memorial Hospital. The nurses were in the early months of their training when the triplets came into their lives. It was the first set ever born at the hospital and they were a real challenge to the staff, as the smallest weighed only three and a half pounds. Esther, who was only nineteen, was allowed to go home two weeks after the birth, but the infants stayed in hospital for three months. This photo shows nurses Hattie Hunter and Ella MacDougall introducing Esther to her babies for the first time as she headed home to recuperate and prepare to look after the babies.

There were no incubators available and the cold of winter days challenged Dr. Garnet Turner and the nursing staff. The babies were kept isolated in a warmed room. Warmed cotton batting was used instead of diapers. "We kept them naked as Jay birds," say the retired nurses who tended them and recall the experience still. "They were finicky to feed because they were so small, so we used medicine droppers to place the milk in their tiny mouths," relates RN Ida (Harvey) Mounce. That was a very slow and painstaking procedure, but very successful, for eventually, Sharon, Shirley and Sheila all thrived and were allowed to go home with their mother at three months of age.

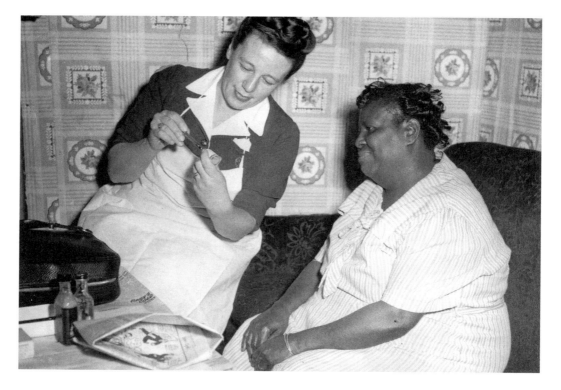

JESSIE DOUGALL, TEACHING DIABETIC PATIENT, 1950

Nurse Jessie Dougall is seen here teaching a diabetic woman how to give herself insulin by sterile technique in her own home. Dougall was both a public health and VON nurse who received her training at the Glace Bay General Hospital before World War Two. She served in the RCAF Medical Corps during the war, and settled in Windsor later.

Female medical workers have long been important to the people of Windsor. Before the hospital was built in 1905, some women specialized as midwives, assisting women and their doctors at childbirth. They were knowledgeable attendants who moved into the homes of women about to deliver and attended to children and household work until the event was complete. One in particular was Agnes Singer, a widow and Scottish war bride of World War One. Doctors did home deliveries at the time, and Agnes offered a room in her home for special cases that doctors knew needed special care around the time of delivery.

Nursing training began in Windsor with the construction of the Payzant Memorial Hospital in 1905. By 1913, the annual student enrolment was significant enough that a student residence was needed, and the community raised the necessary money. A nurses' residence was built in 1914, and served the community until 1976.

Chapter 5

Natural Resources, Industries, and Businesses

BENNETT SMITH'S SCHOONER BLACKWATCH, 1877

John Smith of Newport began building ships in Windsor in the 1820s, and his four sons followed him in the trade. The Smith Yard was on Nesbitt's Island, the most northerly end of Windsor (so named because at high tide it was separated from the rest of town. Earth fill was used to overcome that problem), near the junction of the Avon and Saint Croix Rivers. John's son Bennett became famous for the quality and large sizes of ships that he built. He had a beautiful house there as well as his shipbuilding facility and wharves. The area was actually called Smith's Island at one time. Smith's brother-in-law, Shubael Dimock, apprenticed with him. They had a falling out and parted company. When Shubael Dimock founded his business and shipyard on the shore of the Saint Croix River, just beyond the Smith Shipyard, that area became known as Dimock Point.

Bennett Smith and brothers John and William apprenticed with their father John and carried on the business after his death in 1832. Bennett appears to have been the business tycoon of the three, for by 1836 he owned the yard and business. He was the principal shareholder of the many vessels he built, and they travelled all over the world bringing him great wealth. He usually paid the other shareholders in gold sovereigns from his home following the return of each ship to Windsor. All in all, he built twenty-seven ships. The *Black Watch* was the largest and last ship he built, and was named after the regiment of his Loyalist grandfather Captain John Grant. During the building of *Black Watch*, shown here under construction in 1877, he had a disagreement with his employees of forty-one years. He vowed never to build another ship in Windsor. He then closed the shipyard and moved from his island home near the shipyard to a magnificent new home in the centre of Windsor at the corner of Albert and Plunkett streets. He then had nine ships built for him in Hantsport and Saint John. The *Black Watch* was wrecked on its maiden voyage off of the coast of Scotland. When he died in 1886, Bennett Smith was a very wealthy man with one of the largest fleets of ships in Canada.

A group of Windsor entrepreneurs comprising William Curry, Bennett Smith, Godfrey Philip Payzant, Mark Curry, Edward Wilson Dimock, Thomas Aylward, John Sterling, and William Dimock decided to develop a cotton manufactory and bought land on Nesbitt's Island from three landowners in 1881. By 1884 they had constructed a large brick building and chimney for the power plant. Machinery was imported from England and since nobody in the area was knowledgeable about the industry, a manager and staff were enticed to emigrate to Windsor from England as well. Local people were trained to fill other positions. Dominion Cotton Mills of Montreal bought out the company in 1891, and a downturn in business followed in 1908, causing the mill to close for two years.

The Eureka Woolen Manufacturing Company of Eureka, Pictou County, suffered a serious fire in 1915 and decided to regroup in Windsor. The Windsor plant reopened in 1916 as the Nova Scotia Underwear Company. The company labelled itself as "the Largest Underwear Factory in Canada Under One Roof." Its products were advertised under the Eureka label and claimed "Unshrinkable Nova Scotia Wool."

In 1920, J. E. "Joey" Mortimer, an experienced manufacturer, was brought from England to reorganize the mill. Experienced female workers moved from Eureka to Windsor. Under the direction of Mortimer, the company bought a large house on Nesbitt's Island for the women to live in and named it Eureka Hall. (It had been the home of shipbuilder Bennett Smith, who had sold land for the founding of the industry back in 1881.)

In 1922 the company changed its name to Nova Scotia Textiles Limited, and began to manufacture fabrics woven from cotton, wool, and other materials. The company was under the management of Mortimer until his death in 1956. During that time, the staff worked as a proud unit with camaraderie enhanced by having its own competitive sports teams, including tennis, cricket, baseball, and ice hockey.

THE WINDSOR FOUNDRY, 1890

By 1855, the Dimock Brothers, who had created a ship chandlery business, realized the great need for an iron foundry for making ships' parts, at that time being imported from England at some expense. They built the Windsor Foundry on O'Brien Street and opened a retail store downtown. In addition to making parts for ships, the foundry produced stoves of various sizes and shapes for homes and offices. Their common brands were Base Burners, Acorn, Silver Moon, Ayers, and Windsor. So popular were their stoves that they hired a salesman and expanded the business to supply other parts of Canada. By 1872, business was so good that they dissolved their partnership. William maintained the thriving hardware and ship chandlery, and Edward owned and managed the Windsor Foundry. By the 1890s, both businesses had begun to decline.

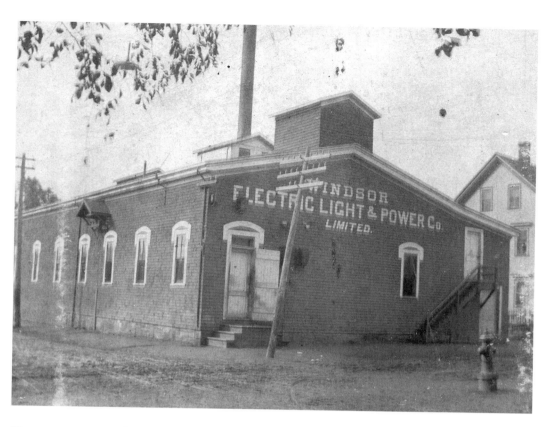

**WINDSOR
ELECTRIC LIGHT
COMPANY, 1890**

By September 22, 1890, electricity was being produced by a coal-burning furnace and generator in a new building at the corner of Stannus and Victoria streets. The gas works, which had supplied gas lighting for streets since 1852, was taken over by the new Windsor Electric Light and Power Company.

In 1892, adequate street lighting was in place and the Windsor Furniture Factory was the first industrial building in town to be lit and powered by electricity. Other businesses soon followed suit and by 1900 homes had begun to adopt electric lights instead of kerosene lamps. Of course, not all families could afford the change, and the conversion to electricity was slow. Well into the 1950s, some houses in town were still dependent on kerosene lamps. A metal smokestack, as shown in the photo, was first used for the "Light Factory," as it was called, but a brick chimney was built later and survived the 1897 fire. It was unharmed and ready to be used again once a new building was constructed and the fire-damaged machinery was replaced. In 1927, the electrical industry was taken over by the newly formed Avon River Power Company. The plant closed out its operations and the building was taken over by Logan Smith, who installed a soda pop factory producing Banner Drinks in the front part of the building. The electric generators remained in place for decades before the building was removed to make room for a storage yard by the Avon River Power Company.

THE CLIFTON HOTEL, LATER THE DUFFERIN HOTEL, 1890

A magnificent-looking building, the Clifton Hotel was conveniently situated on Water Street across from the railway station. It has a very interesting history. James Pellow was working for Thomas Chandler Haliburton in 1848 when gold nuggets were discovered in the American River in California. People from all over the world left for California seeking their fortune. Many became ill and died on the way or shortly after arriving, and not all who got there got rich, but Pellow was one of the lucky ones; he became wealthy. When Pellow returned to Windsor, Haliburton was aging and ready to move to England for his retirement years. Pellow used his new-found wealth to purchase Haliburton's Clifton Estate, which he had so long admired. He carried on Haliburton's gypsum-quarrying and -export business and also built the large and commodious Clifton Hotel. Travellers who had to stay in town overnight as they waited for their ship to come or go on the Bay of Fundy tide were well accommodated at the Clifton. There were several well-appointed shops on the ground level and other businesses overhead, such as Windsor's first weekly and the predecessor of the *Hants Journal*, the *Saturday Mail*.

In 1890, Pellow sold the hotel to John Cox, who had been running the smaller Avon Hotel. John Cox renovated and renamed it The Dufferin Hotel, in honour of Canada's Governor General Lord Dufferin, who had visited Windsor in 1873. The Dufferin Hotel escaped the 1897 fire, but it succumbed to flames in 1905.

BENJAMIN'S LUMBER MILL, 1890

Shipping of lumber by schooners from Windsor began in the early 1800s and became a major industry. Supplying lumber for rebuilding the town in the early 1900s after the Great Fire was big business as well. Samuel P. Benjamin was up to the task. In addition to his mill staff, he employed crews of men to harvest trees from regional forests and others to haul logs by ox teams to the large mill in Falmouth. The crews had to be fed by day and bedded down by night, as did the horses and oxen used in the woods. Benjamin provided a large cookhouse and bunkhouse for the crew and barns for animals. Lumber was carried on scows pulled by tugboat down the west branch of the Avon River to Windsor and points beyond. The S. S. *Parrsboro* had a unique collapsible smokestack that allowed it to pass beneath the Sangster Bridge and Windsor's Twin Bridges on its way to the Bay of Fundy. Benjamin's mill was a very significant business for decades. Benjamin also managed a similar enterprise on the Gaspereau River near Wolfville.

SCHOONER GYPSUM QUEEN, 1891

Built in 1891, the schooner *Gypsum Queen* was the first of the "royal fleet" of schooners of the Gypsum Packet Company formed that same year. The *Queen* was built at Parrsboro and carried gypsum for two decades before being sold for other uses. The fleet carried gypsum from Hants County quarries and the wharf at Wentworth to the J. B. King Wharf at Staten Island, New York. The plant at Staten Island was actually called the Windsor Plaster Mills. J. B. King of Staten Island joined the accounting staff of the Gypsum Packet Company at Windsor in 1891 and became a partner. He was soon president. In complete control of the company, he then acquired the Hobart Wharf at Summerville, where the "royal fleet" underwent repairs. The formerly Windsor-owned company had become a subsidiary of the American Gypsum Company. Soon Otis Wack, an American, arrived to become managing director. He was followed by another American manager, Mike King.

WM. CURRY AND SON WOOD MILL AND FACTORY, 1895

William Curry began this wood mill at Curry's Corner on the Spa Spring Road in 1852. It had a large steam engine to handle lathes, straight and circular saws, and planing and spoke (for wagon wheels) machines. It was a very modern, efficient factory and soon required secondary factories on Thomas Street in Windsor, called the Sash and Door Factory and The Carriage Factory.

In 1890, the business began making caskets and coffins and offering an undertaking service. An ad in the *Hants Journal* read, "We keep constantly on hand CASKETS AND COFFINS, all sizes and styles, and with two Hearses can take charge of funerals promptly and at short notice."

The factories produced wood for the rebuilding of the town following the fire of 1897, and continued producing building materials until after World War Two. The Curry's Corner factory was replaced with a new building for the Ben's Bread Company, while the Thomas Street factory gave way to the Hants County War Memorial Community Centre in 1947.

THE SHAND–CURRY STORE, c.1895

The large white building in this photo was the site of a very significant business leading up to 1897. Partners and brothers-in-law A. P. Shand and Mark Curry began in a general merchandise business in 1859 that served the rural population as well as the town. Many of the farm folks were short on cash but had logs and timber to trade. The barter led to stockpiles on the waterfront premises. Much of the wood was fine oak, and when the stock of wood became too great for trading, the proprietors decided on a clever use of the excess—a woodworking factory. They developed the Windsor Furniture Factory on adjacent Albert Street and began producing home and office furniture. Just as the business began to thrive, the Shand–Curry store and factory buildings were destroyed by the Great Fire. Their homes, high on Ferry Hill, were spared, and rebuilding of the furniture factory began almost immediately. It thrived even more than before because of the mass demand for products to furnish new homes and businesses as the town was reconstructed.

This photo shows the large Shand–Curry Store and tall smoke stacks before the fire. To the right is the base of the boardwalk leading to the highway bridge crossing the Avon River.

BETH SHAND IN WINDSOR'S FIRST GREENHOUSE, 1900

As for so many families, the Great Fire destroyed the business and home of Ezra Shand and his second wife, Augusta, and their two daughters, Elizabeth and Lois. The business was a thriving sash and door factory, but as Ezra went about building a new home, he decided to change his line of work and create Windsor's first hothouse for growing flowers. The retail space was on Water Street, and upstairs was the new home of the family. Behind the store was a second building, which housed a steam-power plant and a workshop. Alongside were two glass hothouses. The front one, parallel to Water Street, was a fern house, and the other a carnation house. Bulk seeds were purchased from England and packaged by Shand's daughters, who worked at the business. When Ezra died, Elizabeth and Lois carried on with the very successful business, eventually selling to H. H. Pulsifer of New Minas in 1946. Fred and Howard Pulsifer, sons of H. H., were in charge of the Windsor operation for many years. In 1965 the hothouses were moved to New Minas and Windsor lost one of its oldest and most colourful businesses.

Gypsum Quarry, near Windsor, N.S.

GYPSUM QUARRY TRAIN CARTS, 1920

In the 1920s, men dug gypsum from the quarries and loaded it into dump carts with picks and shovels. Next, they led the horses and carts to the nearby train carts lined up on narrow-gauge tracks. The train carts were positioned beneath an elevated platform that allowed the rock to fall into place when the dump carts were tipped, without the rock being shovelled again, as was required before such a train was available. The whole process is seen in this photo. When the train was fully loaded, the train's steam engine would appear and haul the collection of carts to the storage sheds at the wharf to await arrival of a ship to take it to market. When the ship arrived, the whole shovelling process was repeated. The method seems archaic compared with today's quarrying technology, but it was state-of-the-art back then.

LOHNES FUNERAL HOME AND HEARSE, 1923

Shown on the right in this 1923 photo is Windsor's first undertaker, Ira B. Lohnes, with his hired driver, Archibald Boyd, near Dodge's Garage at the corner of Albert and Water streets. They are sitting on the town's first hearse.

Prior to 1922 people in the Windsor area, as elsewhere, arranged their own family funerals. Nurses or midwives usually wrapped bodies in preparation for burial and a wake was held at home. Caskets were made by a family member, a friend, a professional carpenter, or purchased from Curry's Mill, which manufactured them and had begun to keep a few on hand at all times. A livery stable operator would supply transportation to the cemetery if the family didn't have a horse and wagon. Lohnes was working at Curry's lumber mill in 1922 when he decided to begin providing a regular service of care for the dead. Wakes were still carried out at home, but the dead were prepared for burial and placed in the casket that Lohnes would supply. The undertaking parlour was at the corner of Gerrish and Grey streets, in a building now used as a Legal Aid Office.

This photo shows the beautiful Avon Falls with the Froth Hole at its base, well known to travellers of Route 14, on the road between Windsor and Chester, into the 1920s. The falls were 125 feet high and spilled over a solid rock face. The water originated from Falls Lake, one of a chain of lakes between the two towns, and ran off through Indian Orchard into the Avon River. In 1919, Roy Jodrey of White Rock and Charles Wright of Wolfville successfully dammed the Stivers Falls on the Gaspereau River to create an electrical power plant for the Wolfville area. It was the first hydro-electric plant in Nova Scotia. They saw the possibility of repeating the performance for Windsor at Avon Falls. W. H. Chase and T. B. Akin invested and became shareholders. K. L. Warren, the engineer from Quebec hired for the Gaspereau Power Plant, did the survey for this one as well. Carl Whitman became resident engineer, and the McDonald Construction Company of Dartmouth was granted the contract to build the dam. Tom Aylward of Falmouth was hired to supply the gravel for the huge amount of concrete required. Being a farmer himself, Tom realized that oxen and horses were required for farm work in all seasons but winter. Therefore, he organized men to use their animals and carts for the job during the winter of 1922, long before trucks were available for such work. Dump carts were fitted with runners and the boxes were made tight so as not to allow gravel to slip out onto the roadways. One man with his cart was assigned to supply snow for the parts of the road that became worn bare. From December to April, gravel was hauled from Shaw's Gravel Pit at Windsor Forks. Since there were not enough local farmers to fill the need, Tom had cookhouses, bunkhouses and animal stalls built and hired men and their teams from Hantsport and Canning areas to live at the camp and work.

In 1924, the Avon River Light and Power Company was established, with adequate power for the town and surrounding area. Businesses and some homes began installing electricity. The company purchased the old Windsor Electric Light Company in 1927, thus taking over the local electric power business entirely. Then, in 1929, the Nova Scotia Light and Power Company bought out several such small companies about the province, including the Avon River Power Company.

HAY TIME NEAR WINDSOR, 1920S

There have been several large farms on the periphery of Windsor ever since the area became inhabited by Acadians. The council grants following the expulsion of 1755 merely changed land ownership from Acadian to English. Indeed, Michael Franklin, who became Lieutenant Governor of the colony, was given a grant that included Nesbitt's Island and a large area of farmland at the base of Fort Edward and along the dyked shore of the St. Croix River toward Halifax. It continued as a farm even into the 1970s.

Eventually the land was subdivided, as immigrants arrived from New England and the British Isles. The process of harvesting hay was far different in those times than it is today. In the 1920s it was still a family affair, with all taking part. Some cut hay with hand-held scythes, while others raked and stacked the hay. A team of oxen and a hay wagon with iron-rimmed wooden wheels was the accepted method of transportation. Workers piled the hay as high as possible on the wagon using pitchforks. The drivers then headed for the barn to pitch the hay high into the overhead door of the hay mow. In this photo, one pitchfork can be seen rising above the farmers on a farm at the outskirts of Windsor. The driver is wearing a lightweight compressed paper "pith helmet" to keep off the sun's rays, while the younger Laurie Hawboldt, who farmed for a living all his life, isn't bothering with a hat on this day. The hay hanging loosely from the wagon shows the method was not nearly so precise as those developed with machines a couple of decades later.

This photo shows the office of the gas works of Windsor. It was located on Nesbitt's Island, beyond the north end of Water Street. The story of how, and precisely when, the town first got early evening street lighting by gas light is intriguing. According to recorded history, Abraham Gesner of Cornwallis (Kentville) developed gas by distilling a solid hydrocarbon called albertite, which he quarried in Albert County, New Brunswick. He was a doctor, scientist, and geologist who tried to promote interest in the gas in Nova Scotia in 1851 but failed to do so. He therefore went to the United States to patent his discovery in 1853. Herein lies the mystery, for in 1852, a group of entrepreneurial men in Windsor set up the Kerosene Gas Light Company on March 31, 1852. Making a connection between Gesner and the Windsor men would be pure conjecture, for no recorded information proves such a relationship. On the other hand, to suggest that the businessmen discovered the gas on their own would be a very great stretch of the imagination.

With permission from the town council "to break open the streets" for the purpose of laying pipes for transporting the gas, the company planted poles with lamps along Water and Gerrish streets and hired a lamp lighter. He walked the route with a ladder each evening at dusk and lit the lamps by climbing up to them. This system worked quite well, and in the 1880s, street lamps stretched from Curry's Corner to the river, a distance of a mile. No record of how the gas was produced can be found. In 1890, the company announced in the *Hants Journal* that the method had been refined and would result in better light. But by then, another plan for lighting had developed. Electric light was being explored, as it was produced in New York. Soon a new industry was founded and the gas works was taken over by the new company. The main building was allowed to deteriorate but the small office was rented as a family home by Robert Sweet and his wife, as shown here in the 1920s.

LOGAN SMITH'S BANNER DRINKS, 1927

During the 1940s, Logan "Loge" Smith was an elderly gentleman about town. He was then operating a secondhand furniture store on Water Street. He seemed to know everybody about town, had a deep, sonorous voice, and sang bass in the Baptist choir and men's quartets as they came and went over the years. He acted in plays sponsored by church and community groups.

What he was best known for, however, was introducing pop to the area in the form of Banner Drinks. Beginning with a small operation on Nesbitt's Island in the early 1920s, Smith moved to the Windsor Electric Light Company building when it was vacated in 1923. His products sold into the 1940s, and were so popular that it was suggested that, had he continued, he might have become highly successful on a national level.

Until 1930 all milk sold in the Windsor area was as it came directly from cows. A decade before, it could be bought by the dipperful on the streets of town as dairy farmers travelled about, peddling it from large containers on open wagons. Next, the dairy farmers bottled it, developed groups of customers and delivered it door to door each morning all year round. The farmers watered, fed and milked the cows, then bottled and delivered the final product. They also separated cream, made butter and sold both as part of their business. Cleanliness and prevention of contamination of product was never under any general program of inspection or control. Any cleaning of the animals or their udders was all left to the integrity of the dairy farmers.

But at that time tuberculosis was extremely common, and when a link between bovine and human strains of the disease was suspected (though not proven), purification by a new process called pasteurization of all milk became popular.

Therefore, when J. D. McKenzie of Middleton established a creamery at Windsor in 1930, it was greeted happily by all concerned citizens. He bought out the business interests of several dairy farmers by promising to buy their milk and pasteurize it. He made it easier for the farmers by purchasing their bottles, wooden carrying cases and delivery wagons. Then he hired several of the drivers to continue with deliveries. Charlie Walker was the plant manager and pasteurization technician and Elmer MacPherson was office manager, with assistants Howard Noiles and June Hergett. Rupert Pemberton, Burpee Caldwell, Had Weatherbed and Russell Clarke bottled milk and cream, Stuart McCann was the butter maker, and Ralph MacPheson, Eric Boyd, and Billy Graham were drivers.

Some people in this and other areas continued to buy milk directly from farms for a while but gradually all switched over to pasteurized products, and bovine tuberculosis gradually came under control all around the world. In the 1950s, the horse-and-cart method of milk delivery in Windsor was replaced with truck delivery to stores and homes.

WINDSOR TRIBUNE PUBLISHING COMPANY, C.1935

The sturdy, handsome, red-brick structure, with a corner entrance at the junction of Water and King streets, was built in 1914. Mrs. Peter Fielding (first name unknown) was an editor of the weekly newspaper. Miss Forbes (first name also unknown) was the office secretary and Ken Miller and Ray Pollard were reporters. Together they produced a weekly newspaper of four to six pages, small pamphlets, booklets, hand-bills, and posters. That was a major achievement for a publishing company in a small town, especially when the newspaper sold for only three cents a copy and had a very limited circulation. Local subscribers enjoyed delivery to their homes by newsboys, while out-of-town folks received their copies by mail. Others purchased copies at any of three drugstores, two bookstores, or Bustin's Restaurant. Newsboys and stores received one cent per copy, leaving two cents for the publisher to cover expenses. The *Tribune*'s competitive weekly, the *Hants Journal* hit the stands on Tuesday and had a much larger following. Cynics said the *Tribune* waited to see what news appeared in the *Journal* on Tuesday, reprinted it on Wednesday, and circulated it on Thursday. True or false, the *Windsor Tribune*, with its own staff, reporters, and fans, served the area for four decades. Editor Kay Anslow of the *Hants Journal*, bought out the *Tribune* in 1955 and amalgamated the papers.

THE COMMERCIAL BANK OF WINDSOR, C.1940

The first bank to be founded in Windsor was the Commercial Bank at the corner of Water and Stannus streets in 1865. The shareholders and directors were prominent Windsor merchants, lawyers, shipbuilders, and ship owners. The first president was Godfrey Payzant, who held the position until his death in 1895. A. P. Shand then became president. The bank burned in the Great Fire and was rebuilt immediately, with a unique feature included in the design: the likenesses of Shand, president, (on the right) and John Keith, vice president, were carved in red sandstone blocks opposite the top of the pillars that supported an arch over the main doorway.

In 1856, a decade before Windsor's Commercial Bank was founded, a Halifax bank was incorporated under the name of the Union Bank. It prospered and soon made overtures to the owners of the successful Commercial Bank of Windsor. In 1902, the Windsor shareholders accepted a deal in which they received shares in the Union Bank and the Commercial Bank was taken over. Meanwhile, the Merchant's Bank formed in Halifax in 1864 and went on to become the Royal Bank of Canada. In 1910, the Royal Bank bought out the Union Bank. The office of the former Commercial Bank at the corner of Water and Stannus streets became the Royal Bank. The building burned in 1961 and the effigies of Shand and Keith were deposited at the West Hants Historical Society Museum.

This photo of the Royal Bank was taken at the doorway of the bank in the 1940s. Back row, l–r: Lewis McCoy, J. J. G. MacDonald, Bertha McCrae; third row: Pauline Mounce, Norma Creed, Erna Shand, Dorothy Cochrane; second row: Margaret Maw, Jean Campbell, Marion MacCarthy; front row: Dorothy Armstrong, Kathleen Dill, Olive Levy, Marjorie Slaunwhite, Gladys Rippey, Helen Baird.

COLONIAL FERTILIZER WORKMEN, 1940

Jim Burbidge, Jim Fraser, Herb Miller, and others are shown with handcarts and shovels.

There are no signs to indicate so today, but Windsor produced agricultural fertilizer in significant quantities for the world market for ninety years. Nicholas Mosher IV, a noted shipbuilder in nearby Avondale, moved to Windsor and began a fertilizer industry in 1885. His partner in business, and manager of the firm, was Robert Pidgeon, who had moved from Saint John. Mosher died two years later, and Robert carried on with the Pidgeon Fertilizer Company. Gwendolyn Shand writes in her *Historic Hants County*, "Four days before the Windsor Fire the barque 'Lizzie Curry' was reported off Hantsport with a cargo of crushed bone from Rosario, Argentina; 600 tons of the cargo were for the Pidgeon Fertilizer Company." In 1912, the plant was purchased by the American Consolidated Rending Company and became the Colonial Fertilizer Company. In 1960, when Lewis Bearne of Windsor was manager, the company was purchased by Canada Packers Ltd. After ninety years of operation, the business was transferred to Port Williams in 1975 and the Windsor plant closed.

FRANK MARRIOTT AND YEAR-ROUND CHRYSANTHEMUMS, c.1940

Frank Marriott is credited with developing the year-round chrysanthemum at Avon Valley Greenhouses between 1935 and 1947. We usually refer to it today as the potted mum.

Marriott came to Falmouth (across the Avon River from Windsor) under the auspices of an English child welfare program that sent disadvantaged children to Canada in search of a better life.

When he died on February 21, 1984, he was a retired production manager of Avon Valley Greenhouses, Falmouth, Nova Scotia. As such, he had a list of accomplishments, not the least of which was that, since 1935, along with his business partners Ralph Loomer and Silas Taylor, he had developed the floral business in Falmouth from four homemade greenhouses, with initial capital of two thousand dollars, into a ten-acre facility with annual sales in the multi-million dollars.

But creating potted mums was his finest achievement. The chrysanthemum had been classed as a fall flower. In the industry it was sold as a cut flower or "spray mum." Then, during the 1940s, by adjusting the carbon dioxide content of the air and using black cloth covers at certain times of the day to control the light on his plants, Marriott was able to grow mums in other seasons. By 1947, he had perfected the method. The results of his experiment caused great excitement all over the globe. Next, in partnership with other Canadian and American growers, he perfected the short-stemmed potted mum, globally popular today.

Frank Marriott's obituary, printed in *The Canadian Florist* magazine, presented the following tribute. "With the death of Frank Marriott, the greenhouse industry of Canada lost one of its foremost horticulturists. A largely self-educated grower, he became a highly skilled individual. He was a perceptive reader, keen observer and creative thinker who reached a stage of professional competence that made him a welcomed consultant with leading horticultural scientists on their own level. He was particularly recognized as a chrysanthemum grower. He pioneered the use of Carbon Dioxide air enrichment to enhance plant growth. He played a key role in international recognition accorded Avon Valley Greenhouses for being the first commercial grower to produce chrysanthemums year around. The first effort was three crops a year but within a few years, more than four crops of spray mums were being produced each year. Chrysanthemums continue to be an Avon Valley specialty."

WILLARD BISHOP AND STATION CFAB, 1946

In 1939 Avard Bishop of Windsor, who was an electrical engineer with the Avon River Power Company and a "ham radio operator," created a so-called "wired" radio station with the assistance of his son, Willard. It hooked up their home on Clifton Avenue with some other homes in the neighbourhood around Ferry Hill, Albert, and Grey streets. While learning electronics from his father, Willard created programs that included music, local news, and amateur plays involving his schoolmates. The programs could be heard only on radios of the "wired" homes.

Then, with the outbreak of World War Two, the government silenced all amateur radio stations and ham operators. Bishop's equipment was seized by the RCMP and removed to Halifax. Meanwhile, Avard and Willard used loudspeakers and microphones to introduce "sound equipment" to their fellow Windsorians at the Windsor Exhibition Grounds, and played Christmas music in the downtown area. In 1945, as the war ended, the Bishops applied for and were granted a licence to create radio station CFAB. By 1948, CFAB had a satellite station at Kentville called CKEN. That system expanded to Middleton and Digby and blossomed into the Annapolis Valley Radio System, serving the entire valley. What Avard and his son Willard started turned into a magnificent radio service worth millions.

In 1997 Willard was inducted into the Broadcast Hall of Fame by the Canadian Association of Broadcasters, following which the Atlantic Association of Broadcasters recognized him as the Broadcaster of the Year. Willard wrote a book, entitled *Likely They Didn't Get The Memo,* in 2000. He was a great Canadian and Windsorian.

Coincident with the sixtieth birthday of Canada, the *Hants Journal* celebrated its hundredth anniversary in July 1967. The town was highly decorated, with arches over main streets, ribbons, balloons, bunting, signs, and flags galore. The Gerrish Street *Hants Journal* office received first prize for the best-decorated building, as shown here.

M. A. Buckley was the first to publish a weekly paper for Windsor on May 12, 1867. He had a small bookshop in the Clifton Hotel. Called the *Saturday Mail*, the paper was produced in his shop and printed in an office upstairs.

In 1875, Charles DeWolfe took over the paper, renamed it the *Windsor Mail*, and moved the office to the upstairs of the Curry Building on Water Street. In 1883, H. A. Nicholson became owner and moved the operation to the upstairs of the Wilcox Building at the north corner of Water and Gerrish streets. He changed the name to the *Hants Journal*, the name of the paper since.

In 1886, James J. (or J. J.) Anslow, who had owned a newspaper in New Brunswick, moved his family to Windsor, having bought out the *Hants Journal*. He opened his new business upstairs in the Blanchard Building. It was from that office that he published editorials pointing out the inadequacy of Windsor's firefighting equipment prior to the Great Fire, which destroyed the office and printing plant.

Anslow was editor until his death in 1914. His son, Harold S. Anslow, then took over the position until he died in 1952, at which time Harold's daughter, Katherine Anslow, became editor. She retired in 1957. David Allbon bought the paper and printing business at that point and carried on. It was Allbon who produced the voluminous Hundredth Anniversary Edition on July 19, 1967. It contained so many old photos and history of the town that it became a keepsake that many people treasure to this day.

Chapter 6

Streets and Stores

DORAN'S VICTORIA HOTELS, C.1880S

The Victoria Hotel has been on Water Street since the late 1700s. Thomas Doran came from Ireland as one of the first immigrants following the Acadian Deportation in 1755. In the oldest photo of the hotel, signs bearing both "Victoria Hotel" and "Doran's Hotel" are seen. It is quite likely that the hotel was called Doran's Hotel originally and later renamed Victoria Hotel in honour of Queen Victoria. Many of the locals continued to call it Doran's for years.

The original hotel was built back a few feet from the street's edge, which gave Doran the opportunity to add a three-storey balcony, shown here, supported by cement blocks. It was constructed and decorated with ornamental woodwork pillars and guard rails on the upper two stories.

LAYING THE CORNERSTONE OF THE FEDERAL POST OFFICE ON GERRISH STREET, 1884

FINISHED POST OFFICE, 1885

Windsor's first post office was a wooden structure at the foot of Burnham's Hill and the corners of King and Water streets. The cornerstone was laid at a great ceremony in June 1884 for a new stone-and-brick building, as was the case in several Nova Scotia towns. The building added greatly to the architectural beauty of the town.

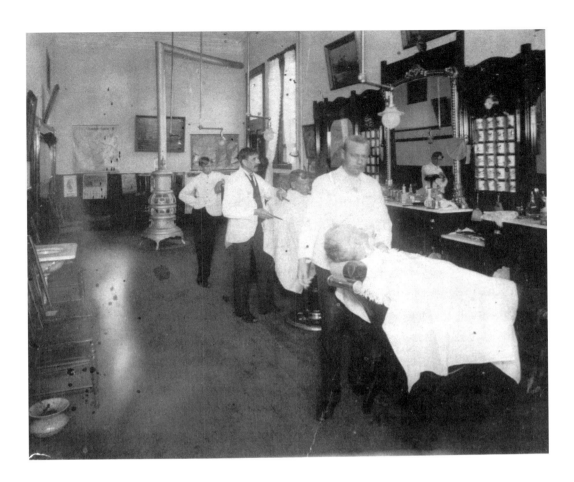

**KIRKPATRICK'S
BARBER SHOP,
1890**

When George Kirkpatrick opened his barber shop in 1890, he started not only a business but an institution in Windsor. He and two employees catered to many regular customers, each of whom had their own personal shaving mug and brush neatly placed on the cabinet shelves between three large plate mirrors facing the hydraulic, padded swivel chairs. Paintings of race horses, dogs, and scenery decorated the back and end wall above the waiting chairs, potbelly stove, and spittoons. A kerosene heater supplied hot water for shaving, which was done with straight razors. Service was supplied to the public from 8 A.M. to 10 P.M. six days a week, and until midnight on Christmas Eve. Kirkpatrick visited clients in hospital and at home if they were too ill to make it to the barber shop.

Barbers worked all year without holiday time, and earned $2 a week in the 1890s, $15 a week in the 1930s, and $45 a week in the 1940s. An apprentice barber cleaned hair from the floor, stoked the fire, and emptied the spittoons as he learned the trade.

Mr. Kirkpatrick retired in 1940 after fifty years at the trade. The building was destroyed, along with the red-and-white barber pole at the door, in order to make way for a new shopping mall and parking lot in 1965.

Water Street ran parallel with the shore of the Avon River and was the heart of the town's business district. Before the Great Fire of 1897, both sides of the street were lined with stores, business offices, banks and telegraph offices, all of wood construction. Driveways between the stores allowed horse- and ox-drawn carts and wagons to access the waterfront wharves that catered to the very busy shipping trade. Two businesses dealing in coal were situated on Water Street, with adjoining storage sheds between streets and wharves. The north end of the street led to Nesbitt's Island with its busy shipbuilding industries facing the water. At the junction of Water Street and the so-called island area was the long and strong forty-foot-high federal government wharf, which was outfitted with railway tracks to accommodate train cars carrying goods to and from ships. It was there that many sailing ships were loaded with gypsum, lumber, and barrels of apples, which made up the bulk of the shipping industry of the area. Also, stores selling dry goods, clothing, animal feed, and groceries, as well as ship chandlers and outfitters and hardware dealers occupied many spaces along the street.

The beautiful Victoria Hotel can be seen on the right side of Water Street in this photograph, majestic in the sunshine. A Printing Office sign hangs above the street beyond the hotel. A small child stands on the sidewalk in left foreground wearing button topped cap and large bow tie. The large boot sign of Dimock's Boot and Shoe Store hangs above the store on the left, while Murphy's sign and another for J. Fred Carver are suspended further along. Every building in the photo was destroyed in the Great Fire.

GERRISH STREET, c.1895

This fascinating old photo shows Gerrish Street. The mortar and pestle symbol seen in the lower right corner was the symbol for an apothecary shop (or a drugstore), R. B. Dakin's shop at the corner of Gerrish and Water streets. The Hants Journal Printing & Publishing House was located above the drugstore until the Great Fire. (The new one, built in 1898, was relocated further up Gerrish Street.) Dan Slack's harness shop was next in line—a very significant business, as horse and wagon service dominated prior to the age of automobiles. Beyond the harness shop is the Gibson Hotel, with flagstone walls and English-style chimney pots.

On the opposite side of the street is E. Percy Webster's jewellery store with a pocket watch symbol hanging from the end of the sign. The next sign is for the Young Women's Christian Temperance Union's coffee rooms. The organization provided the coffee rooms in an attempt to discourage the drinking of liquor.

The post office, of stone and brick construction, is next, and two- and three-storey homes lead towards the Baptist Church in the distance.

Gerrish Street was named for Joseph Gerrish, who received a large grant of land in the central part of town because of his service to England in the France–England wars staged in Nova Scotia. The street extended east from Water Street and for a full block it became an extension of the business district begun on the waterfront with Water Street. Many stores provided customer service and supplies. In addition, the federal post office was built there in 1884, and in 1913 Windsorians raised enough money to add a clock and tower to the building. As automobiles became popular, Wilcox's Hardware Store installed gas and oil pumps by the new concrete sidewalk to service local car owners who still drove on dirt streets. Pavement appeared in the 1920s. The east end of Gerrish Street was residential for three blocks, and ended where it met King Street on its north side and Thomas Street to the south at the Flatiron Corner.

COMMERCIAL BANK OF WINDSOR, 1896

In 1895, John West's cobbler shop stood on the corner of Water and Stannus streets. This photo shows that it was removed and replaced with a new brick building, which was to be the Commercial Bank, later the Canadian Imperial Bank of Commerce. Space for other businesses was planned for the building as well. F. Percy Webster had moved his jewellery business from Gerrish Street into the Water Street side of the new building and hung out his sign. The door to the bank was to be at the corner, and Graham's Grocery Store was established on the Stannus Street side, where the delivery horse and sleigh stand. The brand-new building and everything around it was destroyed by fire in 1897, before the bank became established. In 1898 it was re-constructed in a slightly different form.

**CIVIC BUILDING,
1898**

This magnificent Civic Building was never called such by Windsorians. Rather, it was referred to by the names of its several parts. Built in 1898, it consisted of the town's business office, called the town hall, the fire shed and an opera house.

"The town hall" was the main section inside the single-pillared entrance. It was the centre of town affairs. The town clerk, secretary, and town constable had desks there. Taxes and fines were paid over the high counter just inside the door. There was a council chamber beyond the office as well as a room for the fire department volunteers.

A side door on Gray Street opened to wide stairs that led to the large second-storey space, the opera house. The elevated platform had footlights and a backstage area suitable for professional productions of the day.

On occasion, entertainers arrived from other parts of Canada and the United States to perform, while the opera house was used regularly for important local functions, plays, choral programs, musicals, community orchestral productions, and school concerts and closing exercises. Silent movies were shown there in the early 1900s with a small orchestra in attendance—H. Carleton 'Ky' Smith played clarinet, and brother Sidney Smith played baritone with M. E. Burgoyne on piano. The opera house was the centre of entertainment of Windsor and County of West Hants for decades.

LIVINGSTON'S CANDY STORE, 1900

Wesley Livingston and his assistants supplied the choicest of candies for Windsorians at the turn of the last century and into the 1940s. Pulled molasses candy, sponge toffee, butterscotch lumps, ribbon candy, chocolate-dipped coconut balls and the like were all in great demand. They were on display in the showcases, as shown here, and in the display window, enticing customers into the store. The candy was all made in Livingston's kitchen at the back of the store. In addition to the candy counter, Livingston ran a very popular ice cream parlour on the ground floor and, upstairs, a first class restaurant that also catered to local societies for weekly meeting luncheons. Livingston was also a photographer who recorded local scenery and events. He is seen here with three clerks.

Water Street, Windsor, N.S.

WATER STREET POSTCARD, 1910

Careful study of this photo shows horse-and-wagon teams, an absence of motor vehicles, and an unpaved street. The beautiful buildings are all new, having been built following the Great Fire of 1897. Although the photo was taken in 1910, decades before the invention of colour film, it has been hand-tinted by English photographer James Valentine. The railway tracks that cut through the centre of town can be seen to the lower left, a dog stands near the magnificently designed Blanchards Building, and a man is sitting in front of the equally impressive Geldert's Department Store on the right. The fenced area was to become the site of the Avonian Motors building when automobiles appeared in town.

MURPHY AND DEMONT'S GROCERY STORE, 1910S

People loved this neat and clean store, with its well-stocked shelves and display counters. The hanging electric light fixtures and fine tin ceiling added to the ambience. Clerks at this grocery store retrieved each item a customer asked for, recorded the prices by pencil on a paper bag, added the total, and rang in the payment by hand. The boxes of cereal on the top shelf were accessed by using a broom handle with a bent nail at the top end to tip over a single box. The clerk caught it as it tumbled down and added it to the customer's collection on the counter. A delivery boy was always at hand to carry parcels to the horse and wagon at curb side, or to deliver them by foot to a nearby home.

VICTORIA PARK WAS FLATIRON CORNER, 1910

Victoria Park is bounded by King, Stannus, and Thomas streets. Prior to 1888 it was called Flatiron Corner because of its shape. It contained a pond and swampy area that was connected to a creek that drained into the Avon River on Water Street. The creek was filled in by 1887 and the pond was retained as part of the newly created Victoria Park. Flatiron Pond was used in winter as a place to skate and play hockey for some time thereafter. This 1910 postcard shows the pond as it was at that time, and gives a rare view of the young elm trees planted by a citizen's committee following the fire of 1897.

Note also the metal standard at the junction of King and Gerrish Streets, both of which were still unpaved. It is a water-access station. Long before the town had a general water supply for homes and businesses, there were several places where residents could collect water to carry to their homes. They were natural springs kept clean for people to use. Two outlets can be seen in this photograph on either side of the iron standard.

A. D. Joseph's Store, Scott Block, 1912

William A. Stephens is seen in the door to the left, working as a clerk for A. D. Joseph, who is in the other doorway. Small clothing stores used every available space for presenting as large a stock as possible. The display windows were packed full to entice passers by to come in. Trousers, jackets, winter underwear and coats were often neatly folded and stacked in piles on the floor with just enough space to move around. Most people's clothing looked alike as there were few choices and little chance to purchase items other than from town clothiers. This beautifully appointed and well-kept store was in the Scott Block on Gerrish Street, which burned at night on January 6, 1924 during a snow storm.

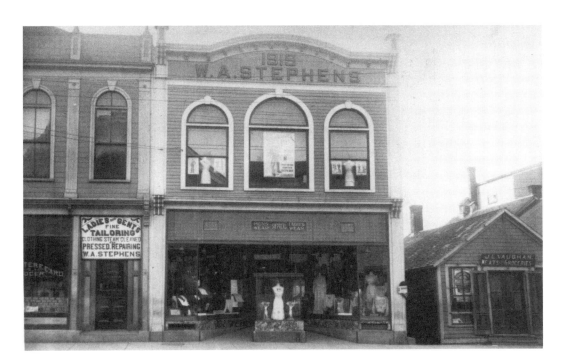

W. A. "Billy" Stephens' Store, 1919

William A. "Billy" Stephens learned his trade as a clerk with A. D. Joseph's store before he began his own tailoring business in a rented upstairs room on Gerrish Street, as seen by the sign over the doorway. In 1919 he opened a clothing store beneath his tailor shop. The business thrived and eventually he took over the buildings on either side of the clothing store as he developed a furniture and appliances store as well. The well-appointed department store had high ceilings and beautifully displayed goods. Stephens was a popular and outstanding citizen as well as an excellent businessperson. He served as a town councillor, school board member, Masonic Lodge member, and firefighter, and he played cornet in the Citizens Band for many years.

J. L. Vaughan, Grocer, Gerrish Street, 1920

The term "small but mighty" applies to this shop. Active throughout World War One, it was popular amongst citizens of the town and the rural district about Windsor. It consisted of the small visible front shop and a larger addition at back. The chicken hanging from a nail in the window moulding was common in butcher shops in Windsor during that era. Rabbits were often displayed in a similar fashion. A small outdoor window shelf offered a few specials of the day.

A careful look reveals iron bars behind the window glass, which indicate part of the story of this historic building. Before it was a meat and grocery store, it was a military jail at Fort Edward. The grocer and butcher, Jimmy Vaughan, eventually sold the building to W. A. Stephens, who moved it behind his clothing store and rented it to Jim Rafuse to use as a mechanic shop.

THE LARGEST STORE IN WINDSOR, 1923

Geo. D. Geldert & Co. employees are busy digging a path for customers to reach the store in this 1923 storm. An 1893 description by Windsor historian George Poole Jones tells about the store: "Dealers in Dry Goods, Gentlemen's Furnishings, latest novelties in Dress Goods, etc.…the largest store in Windsor…furnished with the latest of modern improvements, including cash railway and register, electric light, large plate-glass windows, and the establishment is fitted up equal to the best stores in Halifax and other cities."

WATER STREET IN WINTER, 1923

Automobiles were relatively new in the 1920s, and there were no giant government plows, backhoes, or front-end loaders to clear snow after a storm. When there was an especially big snowfall, as in 1923, store owners had to struggle into their premises to reach their shovels, and then dig a path into the streets beyond. DAR engines had plows on the front of their cow catchers to clear tracks (all old trains had a triangular metal attachment, called a "cow catcher," on the front of the engine to scoop up any animals that appeared on the tracks). They also served to clear a lot of snow for Windsorians, since the track travelled along Water Street and crossed Gerrish and other streets.

Three of the men in the background clearing snow from their premises are Bertram Dimock and Milford Dimock from the tire store, and Raymond Dimock from the boot and shoe store (with the large boot hanging overhead).

ANGLE PARKING
GERRISH & WATER
STREET, 1930S

Windsor stores were open Friday and Saturday nights during the 1930s and 1940s. People from communities around the county, such as Wentworth, Falmouth, Newport, Walton, and Martock, came to town for groceries and other purchases. Gerrish and Water streets were the business district. Shoppers "angle-parked" their cars—as many as five hundred on Fridays and Saturdays—and walked from store to store.

Friday and Saturday nights were also a good time to meet friends and have a chat. The streets were buzzing with people and activity. It was all so interesting that families from Windsor also parked, sat in their cars and watched the sights. In fact, they frequently parked at four o'clock, walked home for supper, and returned to sit in their reserved spot throughout the evening. Children implored their parents to reserve a spot. Windsor boys liked seeing the country girls who arrived in town on those evenings. Perhaps the country girls enjoyed seeing the "townies" too—they never said! The sales of sundaes, root beer, and ice cream floats at the soda fountains of the town's several drugstores certainly increased on those nights!

DODGE'S GARAGE, 1930

Fred Dodge was one of the first Windsorians to sell automobiles. He realized that a mechanic service would be required for his many customers as well, and therefore he opened a garage in the 1920s at the corner of Water and Albert Streets, for the sale and service of Pontiac and Chevrolet cars—both General Motors automobiles. Seen here are two of Dodge's mechanics, Carl Lockhart and Gordon "Hop" Miller, with the firm's accountant standing between them.

FORD TRACTORS FOR SALE, 1950S

Avonian Motors of Water Street often led the Maritimes in annual Ford tractor sales. This photo shows that a new lot had just arrived via the railway station, a mere block away from the business premises. So here are eight of the newest and best tractors, lined up on the street and ready for inspection by the farmers visiting town from the surrounding rural communities.

Chapter 7

People and Homes

THOMAS CHANDLER HALIBURTON, 1840

No account of the history of Windsor would be complete without an explanation of its most famous citizen of all time, Thomas Chandler Haliburton. He gained greater fame and did more for the town than anybody else before or since his time. He was born in Windsor in 1796 and attended King's College School, matriculated at age fourteen, and then graduated from King's College with a Bachelor of Arts. He articled with his father, a lawyer and judge, and became a lawyer himself. Following his father's death, he became a circuit judge at the age of twenty-nine. After twelve years in that position he was elevated to the position of Supreme Court Judge. Haliburton became a member of the provincial legislature in 1826 and stimulated the government to activity that led to an improved highway between Halifax and Windsor. He also organized the building of a covered bridge across the Avon River in 1836, and worked closely with other politicians to establish the railway line between Halifax and Windsor, which was completed in 1858.

But it is not for his political or judiciary efforts that Haliburton is best known. He was also an extraordinarily gifted writer and humourist, and he is known today as both the "Father of Canadian Literature" and the "Father of American Humour." He wrote the first *History of Nova Scotia* in 1829, at the age of thirty-three. Also that year, he created an imaginary Yankee clockmaker, Sam Slick. Slick "wrote" Haliburton's regular column in the Halifax newspaper *The Nova Scotian* (run by his friend and later premier of the province, Joseph Howe), detailing his life as a peddler travelling through Nova Scotian towns and villages, selling clocks to the folks he nicknamed Bluenoses. Haliburton, through Sam Slick, created dozens of what he referred to as "wise-saws"—humorous sayings and phrases. These are still in use today.

Through his writing, Haliburton succeeded in drawing the attention of the people and the government to the needs of the town and province as he saw them.

Haliburton's wife Louisa Neville, whom he married in 1816, died in 1841, a mere five years after they moved into their new home which she had named "Clifton" after her home in England. In 1856, Haliburton retired from public life and left for England to live out the rest of his days.

C. W. Jeffery's illustration of T. C. Haliburton riding with Sam Slick, 1915

Sam Slick's Wise Saws

As quick as a wink
Seeing is believing
He drank like a fish
Real genuine skinflint
I wasn't born yesterday
You're as sharp as a tack
It's raining cats and dogs
A stitch in time saves nine
Barking up the wrong tree
A miss is as good as a mile
They are all uppercrust here
The early bird gets the worm
Facts are stranger than fiction
Give and take, live and let live
This country is going to the dogs
You can't get blood out of a stone
Every dog has his day in this world
As large as life and twice as natural
Six of one, half a dozen of the other
Never look a gift horse in the mouth
What a pity that marryin' spoils courtin'
He flies right off the handle for nothing
I like to let every feller grind his own axe
It's like looking for a needle in a haystack
A nod is as good as a wink to a blind horse
A knowledge of God is the foundation of all wisdom
An ounce of prevention is as good as a pound of cure
A college education shows how devilish little other people know
It is easier to make money than to save it; one is exertion, the other self-denial
If a man seems bent on cheating himself, I like to be neighbourly and help
    him do it

(LEFT)
WILLIAM
ALEXANDER
SMITH, AMOR DE
COSMOS, C.1875

Bill Smith was born in Windsor in 1825 and attended King's College and Dalhousie University. He went to California in 1853 and changed his name to Amor De Cosmos *(lover of the universe)* because he loved beauty, order, and the universe itself. In 1858, he moved north to Canada's west coast and began the newspaper *Victoria Colonist*, in which he criticized the colonial administration of British Columbia just as Joe Howe did in Nova Scotia. He ran for the legislature as a member for Victoria and won, became BC's second premier, and worked toward British Columbia's adoption of responsible government. By 1871, his efforts brought the province into Confederation. He was defeated in the election of 1882 and died at age seventy-two in 1897.

(RIGHT)
REV. SILAS
TERTIUS RAND,
C.1880

Born at Cornwallis (later known as Kentville) in 1810, Silas Tertius Rand was educated at Horton Academy in Wolfville. An ardent student, he mastered the French, Latin, Greek, German, and Spanish languages. He taught school and also worked at his father's trade of bricklaying, while continuing to study. By 1834 he was ordained as a Baptist minister, preaching at Parrsboro, Horton and Liverpool. He became pastor of the Windsor Baptist Church in November 1842 and remained in that position until 1846. While other ministers were going off to foreign countries in the missionary service, Rand created a mission in Windsor, where he preached to the Mi'kmaq in and around the town. He was fascinated with the native culture and lived and worked amongst the Mi'kmaq, eventually establishing a mission in the Hantsport area. He learned their language, worked to improve their condition, and became recognized as "Missionary to the Micmac people."

Fascinated with languages as he was, during his time in Windsor Rand composed a grammar and lexicon of the Mi'kmaw language and translated parts of the Bible for the Mi'kmaq. In 1888 he prepared the *Dictionary of the Language of the Micmac Indians,* which is considered by many to be the authoritative work on the subject to this day.

Interior of old Windsor Post Office.

WINDSOR'S FIRST POSTMASTER, c.1883

Peter Burnham was Windsor's first postmaster. The small, cramped post office was located at the corner of Water and King streets, at the foot of Burnham's Hill, where Burnham lived (it was named after him). Although he looks rather severe in this photo, Peter was a well-known character, genial and full of jokes according to Archdeacon F. W. Vroom, Professor of Theology at King's College, who knew him well. Vroom told of Peter that "When Father Daly left Windsor and moved to Halifax, he took his post office keys with him by mistake. He soon received a postcard with the message, 'Peter is without his keys!' They were promptly returned."

GERRISH STREET HOME, 1890s

This home belonged to a Dr. Moody and was situated at the corner of Gerrish and Grey streets. The glorious architecture and exquisite finishing touches are in sharp contrast to the other buildings between it and the post office, seen in the background. The fancy shingle work, including a striped roof and saw-toothed edges on the dormer-facing shingles, make it distinctive. With the turned posts and multiple spindles on the verandah, plus a finely appointed upstairs balcony, this was one of the finest homes in town. The fine dress of the young girls on the steps is in keeping with the character of the house. The house of Victorian design couldn't have been very old when the photo was taken by professional photographer "I. N. Rice of Windsor and Bridgetown"— the only photo by him in the possession of the West Hants Historical Society. The wires strung across the street and the decorative lamp at the far right show that electric street lighting was in place at Windsor.

CLIFFORD SHAND HOUSE, 1890

No expense was spared and no material denied the craftsmen who built this magnificent home high on Windsor's Ferry Hill in 1890. The design was the newest available from a New York firm named Shoppell's Modern Houses. The furniture and fittings were manufactured at the Windsor Furniture Factory owned by Shand's father, A. P. Shand, and his brother-in-law, Mark Curry. The fancy woodwork on the exterior is believed to have come from Curry's Mill and Curry's Sash and Door Factory of Thomas Street—both equipped to make any type of woodwork required in the area at the time. The property came to be owned by Shand's daughter, Windsor historian Gwendolyn Vaughan Shand, who willed it to the province.

In this photo of the Wilcox house (lower photo) taken in the early 1900s, the new Windsor Academy building and bell tower are seen in the background. Mrs. Wilcox and her daughter Marion are standing on the verandah. The coach house and horse barn are seen at the rear of the property, while a decorative cupola stands on the side lawn.

Andrew Peter Shand and his brother-in-law Mark Curry were partners in business. They built a double house (upper photo) with reverse identical rooms. It was finely appointed with kitchens in "Ls" at the back. The Currys had no children, and when the Shand family began to grow, Mark Curry and his wife built another house nearby and allowed the Shands to take over the entire first house.

BEN GREEN AND HIS SON, C.1900

The significant black population of Windsor and its surrounding region struggled for their survival for many years. Men mostly worked in hard labour jobs, and women often worked as housekeepers. Many have excelled in the fields of education, music, sport, and business, but unfortunately few early photographs of Windsor's black residents survive, and there is little information about their subjects. This photograph is labelled merely "Ben Green and son," and that remains the only information we have about the two.

ANDREW PETER SHAND (L), FRIEND OF WINDSORIANS, c.1905

The name A. P. Shand suggested business success to many people in Windsor at the turn of the century. There was, however, another aspect of the man's life that was much more important to many people both in and far around the town. Shand was a devout Baptist, and contributed greatly to the building of Baptist churches at Windsor, the Plains, Sherwood, and Martock, donating land and materials for the structures. Entrepreneur and philanthropist, Shand frequently took part in church services, even playing the church organ.

ANNIE PRATT (R), c.1910

Annie Pratt developed as a very fine artist, specializing in miniature oil portraits. As with many artists, her ability was not honoured with great sales during her lifetime, but she was supported by a married sister, Charlotte, in whose home she lived at Chestnut Street on Ferry Hill. Pratt suffered an eye injury while in her twenties that ended her career as a miniature portraitist, but she continued with landscape art, and amassed a fine collection now housed at Nova Scotia Archives and Records Management.

Gwendolyn Shand was born in Windsor in 1891. She was educated at the Windsor public school and received a BA from Acadia University. Gwendolyn's grandfather was A. P. Shand, noted Windsor entrepreneur and philanthropist. Her father, Clifford Shand, was a businessman and a champion Nova Scotia cyclist, who introduced the bicycle to the Windsor area. Gwendolyn's mother, Henri "Heni" Shand (née Vaughan), was very supportive of her children, Gwendolyn and Errol, and in close touch with community developments. While Gwendolyn Shand was away at university, she wrote to her mother every day. Those letters are at the Acadia archives and have not yet been published.

After Acadia, Shand studied at London, England, and McGill University. Then, with an MA in social work from the Carnegie-Mellon University in Pittsburgh, she became a social worker amongst the poor of Pittsburgh during the 1930s. She returned to Nova Scotia in the 1940s where, as an executive director of the Welfare Council of Halifax, she improved the social welfare program of the city through the years of World War Two. She became a founder of the Maritime School of Social Work.

Shand had a very keen interest in life and devoted herself to the welfare of others. All of this filled her mind with many exciting memories, which she was later able to preserve in writing. While she had much information about her family and her own busy, productive life that she could have written about, she chose instead to record the history of business and industry in her hometown and county, publishing the still-popular *Historic Hants County* in 1972 to the delight of many. Shand died in 1982 at the age of ninety-one, and the fine Victorian Shand House is now a treasured part of the Nova Scotia Museum.

THE RAFUSES IN CARS, 1909

The couple shown in the new 1909 Hupmobile are James Rafuse and his first wife, Gladys, both of Windsor. The children in the small automobile are their daughters, Eva and Gladys. Rafuse bought the large car but made the small one himself. It seems incredible that he could create such a fine replica of the real machine without the facilities of an automobile factory. So ingenious was his achievement that *Popular Mechanics Magazine* had an article about it in September 1912 issue, and the Nova Scotia Technical College honoured Rafuse for his achievement with an engineering certificate.

Rafuse had two businesses. One was the manufacture of rattan furniture, for which he hired a staff to operate his small factory; the other was a mechanical repair shop, which he ran strictly by himself. For most small jobs, the standard fee was twenty cents. That insured two things: he would never become rich, and he would always have work.

Rafuse was noted throughout the province for his mechanical genius. As evidenced by the photo of him and his second wife, Eva, he somehow managed to set his camera up with a delayed "clicking" mechanism. How he accomplished that in the 1920s remains a secret. It was well established that if a bank vault became stuck and could not be opened, the manager would call in Jim who figured out the lock combination and opened the door.

EVA AND JIM RAFUSE CAMPING OUT, 1920S

In the 1920s, Rafuse built a second car, smaller and far different than any other ever to appear in Windsor or anyplace else. He put it together from spare parts. As bendable plywood was invented, he took advantage of it to build a body over a hardwood frame for his homemade car. Windows were plate glass, door handles were of his own construction, and the engine cap bore his initials, meticulously cut from metal. It was a small coupe-style car, barely big enough for two. There was a carrying trunk in the back of the cab for parcels and groceries, and Rafuse often delighted small neighbourhood children with a ride in the trunk. He and his wife used the car regularly for weekend picnics and fishing trips. As demonstrated in one of his photos, Jim even made a portable canopy for the side of the car, similar to those used on modern motor homes.

The car served the Rafuses for three decades. When it became possible to start motors with a simple turn of a key, Jim was still standing in front of his car using a hand-operated crank to start the engine. In the 1940s when he parked his car and climbed out to saunter into a store, folks would gaze in amazement at the squat, hand-painted light blue car. As Rafuse grew old, slow, and graceful along with his homemade automobile, he prepared a message about both him and his car, for all to read and heed. Across the top of the narrow rear window, he placed a hand-painted sign with fine lettering that read "Don't Laugh, You May Be Old Yourself Some Day".

**MI'KMAW
ENCAMPMENT,
EVANGELINE
BEACH, 1920s**

This photo shows an unidentified Mi'kmaw family at the edge of the woods near Evangeline Beach on the Minas Basin, a short distance from the place originally called Pesegitk—Windsor. A child is handling strips of split ash used for weaving baskets. The family is likely making utility baskets, which were sold to people in the Annapolis Valley. Mi'kmaw basket sellers usually travelled by DAR in the baggage car at half-fare. One woman and a young girl would go from door to door with a large white bed sheet tied at the corners and filled with baskets. The sheet would be opened and contents displayed at each door.

CASTLE FREDERICK, c.1920

An Acadian named Pierre Landry owned a large well-developed farm at Piziquid on the west branch of the Avon River at the time of the expulsion in 1755. The Landry land was granted to an English Naval Officer named J. F. W. DesBarres in 1764 when the area became known as Falmouth, on the outskirts of Windsor. Having passed down through subsequent generations, it now belongs to a descendant, James Bremner who continues using the land in the farming tradition.

Joseph Frederick Wallet DesBarres was a Huguenot, born in 1721, raised and educated in Switzerland. As a young man, he went to England's Royal Military Academy and became an officer, engineer and surveyor. He was destined to become an outstanding cartographer, colonial administrator, wealthy Nova Scotian landowner and noted lover.

At the time of the Seven Years War (1756–63) between France and England, he served with General Amherst at the Siege of Louisbourg (1758) and Gen. Wolfe at Quebec (1759), and contributed greatly to the recapture of Newfoundland from the French (1762). As an engineer, he contributed to the defence of Halifax with the construction of a timber and iron boom at the opening of the Northwest Arm. Following this, he began surveying the east coast of North America and produced the *The Atlantic Neptune*, a series of accurate surveys and charts that has become a classic in marine studies.

For his contributions to the British cause, he was granted land in Falmouth, Chignecto and Tatamagouche. The Falmouth property was the five-hundred-acre Landry Farm that he developed into "Castle Frederick". There, during winter months for eight years, he used material gathered in good weather to form the classical *Atlantic Neptune* charts. Castle Frederick was a significant operation consisting of forty-two men, thirteen women, thirty-three girls, and five boys. Ten of the men were Acadian prisoners loaned from Fort Edward to work the farm. One woman was Mary Cannon, DesBarres' common law wife, known to local people as Polly. By the time DesBarres left for England in 1773, he and Cannon had produced five children.

In England, he found a new woman, Martha Williams, with whom he lived for eleven years, during which time they produced eleven children. He also published the *Atlantic Neptune* during that time, and returned to Halifax in 1784. He became Governor of Cape Breton in 1785. Rather than Louisbourg, he picked Spanish Bay as the capital, where he established a new English settlement and changed its name to Sydney. He lost his position as governor two years later and returned to England. In 1804 he was appointed Lieutenant Governor of Prince Edward Island and remained in that post until age ninety, when he retired to private life in Amherst and then in Halifax where Martha Williams joined him from England. He ignored Mary Cannon except to file a lawsuit against her for alleged mismanagement of his funds at Castle Frederick while he was in England. The case was never settled, nor was his estate of Nova Scotia landholdings, for which his children with Martha Williams spent their money battling in courts. DesBarres died in Halifax at age 103.

JOHN FREDERICK HERBIN, C.1920S

John Frederick Herbin, who called himself "the last of the Acadians," deserves recognition as a very significant Windsorian. He must also be recognized as Windsor's strongest attachment to the Acadians, who were driven from the very place where he was born and raised two generations later. His mother was Mary Robichaud, a granddaughter of one of the exiles from Grand Prè. Following the deportation, her family returned to live at Metaghan on St. Mary's Bay. John's father was a French Huguenot jeweller, who with his young wife made a home in Windsor, where John was born on February 8, 1860. There his mother Mary told him tales of the long struggle of her grandparents to maintain their homes and lifestyle, and of their eventual expulsion. John became passionate about his ancestors at a very early age and his concern developed into a magnificent plan to remember them and their history.

At age nine, John had to leave school and work with his father as a watchmaker in order to help support the family. His parents eventually separated, and his father moved to Colorado. John followed him at age twenty-one. He learned Spanish and worked as a teacher for two years, and on the death of his father returned to the land of the Acadians. He settled in Wolfville, working as a jeweller and graduating from Acadia University in 1890. A year later, at age thirty, he published a book entitled *Canada and Other Poems*, dedicated to the Acadians, and commended by Bliss Carmen. Nova Scotia writer Silas Tertius Rand, noted for his wonderful "word pictures," called some of Herbin's poems "delicately carved cameos."

John married Minnie Rounesfell Simpson, from a colonial family, and they began raising their family. He continued working as a jeweller and became an optometrist of note as well. He also served as a councillor, fire chief, and mayor of Wolfville. And all the while he explored the lands of Grand Pré, where he soon discovered the buried stones of the church of St. Charles, where the proclamation had been read to the Acadians prior to their deportation. With the help of a friend, he used church stones to construct a memorial cross, which remains to this day. Next, he raised enough money to secure the acreage around the church and Acadian grave yard. Before long, American interests contemplated developing the area into a commercial tourism site, based on the popularity of Longfellow's poem, *Evangeline*. Herbin resisted their offers and eventually convinced the Dominion Atlantic Railway to purchase the land and develop a beautiful memorial park. The agreement also arranged the acquisition of land by the Acadian Society for reconstruction of the church, which was to house the artifacts Herbin had retrieved from the area. The park secured the memory of the Acadians on the very site of their home village at Grand Prè, and brought John Herbin's great dream to fruition.

On December 29, 1923, Herbin went out for his regular evening walk on the dykes built by his ancestors. When he failed to return, his family went in search and found that he had died suddenly from heart disease on an old Acadian trail a short distance from home.

In recent years, grateful Acadian descendants have applied a bronze plaque to the memorial cross at Grand Prè, to the honour of John Frederick Herbin.

**JOHN A. DUNLOP,
1922**

As a young boy, John Dunlop emigrated with his family from Ireland in 1904. They lived in Falmouth, where the Dunlop children got their early education in a one-room school before crossing the Avon River to attend Windsor Academy. Like many other young Windsor boys, John and brother Bill joined the army and went overseas in World War One. On returning, they enrolled at Dalhousie, to study law. In 1922, John won a Rhodes Scholarship and sailed for England and Oxford University. Since he had excelled in football, basketball, and ice hockey at Dalhousie, he became a member of the University Hockey Club. As the team's star goaltender, he helped the Oxford Blues win the coveted Spengler Cup.

At the end of his three-year scholarship he returned to Canada, and then joined a corporate law firm in New York. He had only one client in his entire and highly successful career, which he managed from the New York office. Once, he flew out to Burbank, California, for a short while and assumed the position of CEO of his client company in order to save the company from bankruptcy. Once that was settled, he returned to his New York office and continued to manage the affairs of his sole client from there. His client, Paramount Studios, is still in business to this day.

SAM MACDONALD, TOWN COP, 1920S

Windsor had at least two famous "Sams" over the years and their homes were only a pond apart. Sam Slick was T. C. Haliburton's fictitious character, while Sam MacDonald was real. MacDonald was Windsor's policeman for three decades until the 1930s, before the town began hiring a member of the RCMP. A large, impressive-looking man, MacDonald was known as a stern, fair, and respected law enforcer. Whether the problem was a drunk and disorderly person on the streets or a fight amongst the crowd at a hockey game in the old Stannus Street rink, MacDonald was the man to take charge and bring law and order to the scene. His home was beside the abandoned Haliburton gypsum quarries. Since the quarries flooded and froze each winter, providing for great skating and ice hockey, MacDonald became custodian of the ice as well as the town. The large pond was even named after him—MacDonald's Pond. Little wonder that his two sons, John "Chook" and Samuel "Sammy" MacDonald became great players with the town's senior hockey team, which won the provincial championship in 1922 and 1923.

KATHERINE "KAY" ANSLOW, THE TOWN'S FIRST MISS WINDSOR, 1929

A woman of many accomplishments during her ninety-three years, Kay Anslow was a stellar Windsorian from childhood. Born in 1911, she became a local star in sport, music, education, and journalism.

In 1931, Anslow became the first Miss Windsor. She had a keen sense of community and took part in numerous fundraising concerts. During the mid to late 1930s she was director of the Elmcroft Playgrounds for children and choir director and soloist at the Windsor Baptist Church. In the 1930s, she established a school of business at King's College School that included girls, thus introducing co-education to KCS. She founded the Windsor School of Business in 1942, which was responsible for the education of countless young women and men who then held major positions in business locally and elsewhere. During World War Two, she organized the Windsor Concert Party, made up entirely of talented Windsorians, which entertained members of the armed forces locally and around Nova Scotia.

Anslow's grandfather, journalist James J. Anslow, took over the *Hants Journal* in 1886. Her father, Harold S. Anslow, was editor from 1914 until 1952, at which point Kay took over. In 1955 she bought out her competitor, the *Windsor Tribune* and amalgamated Windsor's two weekly papers. In 1957, she sold the *Hants Journal* and felt that she had retired—but she was encouraged to join the staff of the Windsor Regional High School as Head of Business Education. She retired from the position in 1972 but continued to collect historical data of people and events in the Windsor area.

In retirement, Anslow was awarded the Phyllis R. Blakely Lifetime Achievement Award for collecting and recording local history. Well into her eighties, she was still assisting people with their family genealogical research from her vast files. She donated her historical treasures to the West Hants Historical Society.

Harry "Had" Fogarty was born at Windsor in 1901. For five decades, until his death in 1983, he was a barber. Between 1930 and 1950 Fogarty and his wife, Mildred, or "Mid," had ten children who, in addition to their schooling, also got an education at home in music and physical training. The Fogarty parents were great singers, and four of their children became musical entertainers.

The family lived in a two-storey house that had an attic that housed the only private gymnasium in Windsor. There, Fogarty would spar with his sons and friends as well. The children recall being encouraged to use hand-grips, a homemade rowing machine, heavy lifting equipment, and a punching bag. Meanwhile, in the back room of his barber shop on Gerrish Street, there was a small boxing ring. Buster Paris, a customer, remembers getting down from the barber chair and being invited to step out back and spar for a few rounds. For several years at the Hants County Exhibition Fogarty arranged and refereed boxing matches on an elevated outdoor platform. He began his notable baseball career as a pitcher, then moved to left field and spent his senior years as an umpire. While he didn't play hockey, he did contribute greatly as a trainer, long before other towns had thought of the need for such a thing. During World War Two, he organized and managed the Windsor Spitfires senior hockey team in the town's commercial league. In the post-war era, he served as trainer for the Windsor Maple Leafs in the Valley Senior League for several years.

In the barber shop Fogarty carried on continuous friendly sports chatter with his many customers, who got play-by-play descriptions of recent games as well as hot tips as to how best to stay in shape. His lively step and congenial manner as he walked to and from work each day were his identifying features. For many years he carried a small suitcase as he walked across the ice to the players' box at the Annapolis Valley rinks. Jim Wilcox, who long played for the Maple Leafs, explained that Fogarty kept lemon wedges, a terrycloth towel and ice cubes within. They were used to resuscitate injured players when they were down on the ice. Wilcox can recall how quickly a player would respond to a squirt of bitter lemon juice in the mouth or a slap with a frigid, ice-packed towel on the forehead or the groin—wherever it was most needed.

HARRIS HARDING "HARRY" REID, 1940S

Harry Reid was well known as a professional photographer in the Windsor area from the 1920s to the 1960s. He was also an actor, elocutionist, storyteller, writer, poet, fisherman, hunter, violinist, and singer. At Christmastime his voice was heard on the local radio station, CFAB, as Santa Claus, reading letters sent to him from local children who loved to hear him mention their names on the air. On CBC Radio he played the part of Sam Slick in stories of Windsor's famous Judge Thomas Chandler Haliburton. He is shown here with a Sam Slick clock and his old Royal typewriter, composing copy for the CBC in the 1940s.

CHARLIE WOOD AND STAR OF THE SEA PROJECT, 1940s

Charlie Wood was a manual training teacher at Windsor Academy and a tireless community worker. Parents and children alike appreciated his volunteer efforts at the Baptist Sunday School and the Elmcroft playgrounds. He was very active in the Masonic Lodge and other community organizations and initiatives. In addition to the great service to his community, he made a contribution to the fishing village of Terence Bay that had an everlasting beneficial effect.

When the people of Terence Bay, on Nova Scotia's South Shore, were destitute in 1938, Charlie Wood came to their aid. The *Halifax Herald* noted of the people at that time that "hunger, hardship and illness are their constant companions." They lacked food, fuel, clothing, and medical attention. Isolated on a granite-bound coast, and attempting to recover from the Depression, they had suffered an additional community-crippling blow because of an unexplained decline in the fishery. The Sisters of Charity stepped in to help with plans for recovery. Likewise, men who were skilled at training others to do woodwork came up with a plan. Since the women of the village had been accustomed to making clothing for their families and the men had long met the challenge of carpentry in building homes, boats, oars, fish stores, wharves, and buoys, plans for recovery were based on these skills. The Sisters of Charity in Halifax set up classes and taught weaving to women and girls over fourteen. George Day and Arthur Patton, two manual training instructors from Bloomfield High School in Halifax, and Wood went to the village regularly and taught men and boys over fourteen to make utility items and toys. Wood also raised funds to purchase tools and materials, then travelled the province and found markets for the finished products.

Before long the community was producing hand-woven items and woodwork under their own label and trade mark, Star of the Sea. Simpsons and Eatons stores began advertising wool scarves, neckties, and tweed cloth for clothing and drapes made by the women. Stepladders, stools, ironing boards, ashtray stands, bird houses, and toys were made by the men and boys and finished by women and girls. The wooden articles became popular sales items at various stores. By 1948, a decade after the plan was put into effect, Star of the Sea products were selling across Canada, and a special event was held by Mills Brothers of Halifax featuring Terence Bay's Star of the Sea products.

When Wood died of cancer, the many groups and organizations with which he had been associated all around the province joined in a funeral march of respect that is said to have been unequalled in Windsor before or since.

BOB HUGGINS, 1946

It didn't matter if he was announcing a tug-of-war match at the Hants County Exhibition, a Valley Senior League Hockey Game, or a Maritime Baseball Championship game, Bob made it as exciting to radio fans as if they were there. He began his career as a sports announcer in 1946 with radio station CFAB in Windsor, and stayed with the fledgling station as it expanded to the Valley's twin stations CFAB and CKEN under the name Evangeline Broadcasting System (EBC). By then he was so popular that he was enticed to join CHNS in Halifax to begin announcing Maritime sports events. Bob was a natural and thrilled sports fans in all seasons as he brought play-by-play accounts to their homes and rounded off each day with a regular evening sports summary, always ending with, "It's not whether you win or lose, it's playing the game that counts!" In the 1960s the CBC Radio hired him for Canada Games broadcasts, which furthered his career.

Chapter 8

Sport and Recreation

LAWN TENNIS, 1884

M r. Millwood, who came from England to be the first manager of the Windsor Cotton Mill, introduced lawn tennis to Windsor in 1884. This photo was taken at Windmill Hill, the site of Windsor's first tennis courts. The elevated viewing stand preceded multi-row bleachers common after that time. Court lines were "dusted" with chalk or lime onto the grass before "pin-down" cloth tapes were used. Clay courts followed the lawn courts some years later. Paved courts were not considered until after roads were paved in the 1920s.

BICYCLES IN WINDSOR, C.1895

Bicycles that came to Windsor and elsewhere in the late 1860s were experimental versions. The very first was named a velocipede and a driver was called a velocipedist. The nickname of the cycle was "the boneshaker." People in Windsor learned to ride them in the loft of a sailmaker's shop on Water Street, and they soon were holding races in the old Avon River covered bridge, with noises echoing out the open ends.

Clifford Shand of Windsor, shown here with his wife, Henrietta, was a bicycle enthusiast from the beginning. When he entered an all–Nova Scotia championship in 1887, his win started him on a series of fifteen firsts in five years. He acquired a special American-made version of the high-wheeler, a "Star Safety" bicycle, which reversed the positions of the wheels for better stability and control of steering.

There was great public interest in bicycles in the 1890s and the new industry Bicycles that came to Windsor and elsewhere in the late 1860s were experimental versions. The very first was named a velocipede and a driver was called a velocipedist. The nickname of the cycle was "the boneshaker." People in Windsor learned to ride them in the loft of a sailmaker's shop on Water Street, and they soon were holding races in the old Avon River covered bridge, with noises echoing out the open ends.

Clubs were formed, like the Windsor Avonians. Members went for long club rides together, to places such as Saint John and Halifax. Men usually wore skin-tight trousers, boots, a shirt and tie, and a small skull cap with a bill. Women generally wore a blouse, a sweater, and full skirts, which were protected by the wheel and chain guards. They commonly wore a flat, narrow-brimmed decorated hat. Club members got special rates at hotels and on railways.

SWASTIKA HOCKEY CLUB, 1908

The swastika is now indelibly linked with the atrocities of World War Two, and it is strange to see young men wearing the symbol without knowing what it would later be used for. To the Swastika Hockey Club, which existed from 1900 to 1920, the symbol represented good luck—and good hockey.

The team played in the Annapolis Valley Senior League and travelled to Newfoundland by train and ferry boat for an annual ice hockey tournament. By 1908 they had both dark and light uniforms for use at home and away. Their sticks were all one-piece creations, handmade by Mi'kmaw carvers of the province and distributed by The Starr Manufacturing Company of Dartmouth. In this photo, none of the players are wearing "hockey gloves," as they were recently new to the game and few players possessed them.

Back row: Walter Regan, Roland G. Morton, Clarence McCann; centre row: George McKinley Geldert, William Stephens, C. L. Johnson; front row: W. E. McMonagle, Frank Sharpe, Gerald McElhiney

POVERTY POINT RAGGEDY ASS CRICKET CLUB, 1910

In the late nineteenth century, those who built ships at Nesbitt's Island called the area "Dimock's Point" in honour of Shubael Dimock, a Windsor master shipbuilder. In the early 1900s, teenage boys who lived on Nesbitt's Island called their area of town "Poverty Point," because families living there were often very poor. The boys had a cricket club, which they named appropriately— Poverty Point Raggedy Ass Cricket Club, or PPRACC.

Ernie Mosher was a member of the team and went on to become an outstanding hockey player, leading the Halifax Wolverines to Canada's Allan Cup Championship in 1935. The author's father, Jim Vaughan, and Mosher were childhood friends and Mosher treasured this photo of their team. Mosher was able to identify all but one of his young teammates.

Cricket was popular with all ages in Windsor at the time. A rather famous adult Windsor team that competed with Valley and Halifax teams was called the Three Elms Cricket Club. It was so named because the field was at the edge of King's College property, where three giant elms then stood.

Back row (l–r): Everett Kuhn, Fred Kuhn, Harry Hoyt, Jim Vaughan, Don Smith; front row: unidentified, Avard "Rice" Baird, George "Pork" Smith, Ernie Mosher

**VICTORIA PARK
BAND CONCERTS,
C.1910**

In 1908, the pond at Flatiron corner was filled in and a bandstand constructed where the pond had been. The central part of town thus took on a brand new appearance and became Victoria Park, far more useful as an area of enjoyment. Thanks to James Valentine, the famous postcard photographer, we have this reminder of the appearance of both the park and bandstand in 1910. Band concerts became very popular in the park and were held on summer evenings throughout the week and on special occasions. Often visiting military bands took advantage of the facility to perform while in town. James Rafuse, a local craftsman, made ten hardwood benches, so that citizens could sit as they enjoyed the concerts. Mostly, people meandered along the sidewalk that surrounds the park.

Bandstands made of wood have a limited lifespan, and when this one was replaced, the new one had a roof and seats for the bandsmen. By the 1930s, regular concerts were being held by the Windsor Citizens Band on Sunday evenings in good weather. By then, several people owned cars, and would sit in the comfort of their car, listening to the concert and observing the sights. Walking along the sidewalks as the concert proceeded became a common thing for youth to do. Many romances began at Victoria Park during band concerts.

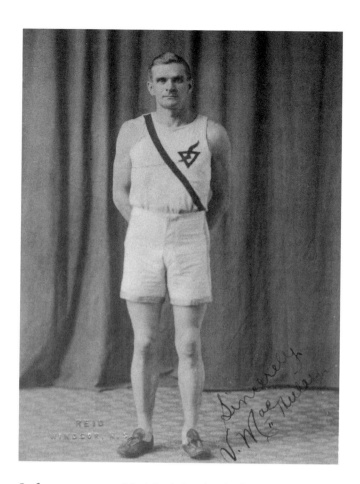

VIC MACAULAY, MARATHON RUNNER, C.1920

So fast a runner was Vic MacAulay that he frequently finished races as much as a half-mile ahead of his followers. So consistent a winner was he that his fans nicknamed him "The Impossible Loser." After a race in Kentville in 1914, the *Hants Journal* reported, "In a ten mile race at Kentville, Victor MacAulay captured first place, having a lead of two miles over his nearest competitor." He found shorter races easy and set a record for the five-mile race at the Antigonish Highland Games in 1922 and again in Pictou in 1923. Mostly he loved longer races, and won the *Halifax Herald* ten-mile marathon in 1912, 1913, and 1914. The successive wins allowed him to keep the trophy. That put MacAulay in the Nova Scotia Sports Hall of Fame, where his trophy is on permanent display. He became known as the top ten-mile runner in Canada, and won the Boston Marathon in 1916. He won the *Halifax Herald* Marathon again in 1921, 1922, 1923, and 1924. At the Olympic Games in Paris, France in 1924, he came in 11th out of 387 runners. MacAulay worked as an auto mechanic for many years during and after his running career. For many of those years he boarded at the Martock House on Albert Street. After a hard day's work, he would return to the Martock House, change into his running outfit, and take off across the Avon River Bridge for a "fun run" before supper. Eventually he developed shortness of breath from emphysema and lived his final days in a Windsor nursing home.

EDGEHILL SCHOOL PICNIC AT LONG POND, 1920

Along with the youth of the Town of Windsor, Edgehill and King's students used Long Pond all year round throughout the 1800s and in the early 1900s. Archdeacon F. W. Vroom and author T. C. Haliburton told of winter activities on Long Pond, as it became a favourite ice surface for "skatists" and "hockeyists," as they were called in the better part of the nineteenth century. In the 1920s, Windsor author Henry Blanchard wrote of town children using it as their favourite swimming place from early spring until fall.

In the late 1700s the pond was a gypsum quarry belonging to John Clarke. When he sold sixty-nine acres of land for the founding of King's College in 1788, the quarry was included. Unused as a quarry from then on, it filled with surface water and formed a pond nine hundred by two hundred feet in area, and fourteen feet deep. In 1842, the college governors bartered with their neighbour, Haliburton, for land that allowed them to build a road from the back of the college to the centre of town, thus saving a one-mile walk from the front of the college on College Road. Included in the trade were a large field that had been the Three Elms Cricket Field (now Clifton Avenue Extension) and an adjacent field containing the Long Pond.

Around 1923, the historically significant Long Pond mysteriously disappeared. Geological "sink holes" developed in the old quarry, and the pond suddenly went dry. Students from Edgehill and King's Collegiate, as well as town folk, lost their favourite picnic spot and swimming, skating, and hockey pond.

But the loss of Long Pond was not a problem for long; Windsor was blessed with a myriad of ponds for both skatists and hockeyists, and there had, since 1870, been a covered rink on Fort Edward.

WINDSOR,
THE PLAYGROUND
OF HALIFAX, 1920

As soon as the English first took control of Pesegitk and renamed it back in 1764, Windsor became known as the "Playground of Halifax." The lakes were alive with trout, the woods with deer and moose, and the sky with wild fowl. Folks came from the city to partake of the wonderful hunting and fishing as well as to play sports with crack teams. Shown here in 1920 are three young men who had returned as army veterans from World War One two years previously and began a new life of work and friendship in their hometown. Bill Mounce, Jim Vaughan, and Harold Smith (l-r) were veterans from Nova Scotia's 112th Overseas Battalion, but quickly put thoughts of war campaigns out of their minds when they fished at Panuke Lake, their wonderful wooded refuge, only a few miles from town. Garwin Smith is standing with his proud father, while Raymond Smith stands watching, as his own father Cliff Smith, another veteran and member of this sporting gang, takes the photo that would forever prove the size of the trout they had caught.

VETS BASEBALL TEAM, 1921

Most of these young men had just returned from overseas duty in World War One. They had played baseball together before going over and weren't long getting a team organized in 1919. What better name for the group than the Vets?

Back row (l–r): Charlie Wigmore, George Robertson, Hadd Fogarty, Andrew Mounce, Harry Smith; middle row: Murray Singer, Cliff Smith, Charlie Smith, Rev. Canon Andrews, Herb Murral; front row: Charlie Black, Allen Singer, Bill Singer

WINDSOR HOCKEY CLUB, 1923

They looked nothing like the well-dressed champions of today but they were good hockey players just the same. Having beat out all competition in the province to become champions of the Nova Scotia Senior Hockey League, the club members were at Antigonish to meet the Abegweits from PEI for the Maritime Championship and the Starr Trophy. Unfortunately the team lost to the Charlottetown Abbies.

Standing (l–r): Frank Poole, Vic McCann, Sam MacDonald, Bert Ryan (mgr.), John MacDonald, Frank "Gunner" Clarke, Ernie Mosher; seated: Pork Smith, Doggie Kuhn, Johnny Hughes, Paddy Rafuse

The members of the women's bridge club played bridge at one another's homes throughout the 1930s and 1940s, and occasionally dressed up for the sheer fun of it. At a time when there was little means of entertainment in Windsor, bridge clubs were very common and important to both men and women.

Back row (l–r): Louise Dimock, Jennie Rockwell, Marguerite Rockwell, Ms. Ewan, Grace Forrest, Florie Taylor, Mary Graham, Ms. Churchill, Valentine Parsons; front row: Ms. Rippey, Anne Allen, Marion Wilcox, Bea Strong, Maud Rowe, Blanche Lockhart, Eva Christie; centre front: Jean Fielding

Back home in Windsor, this team of experts poses for an official Harry Reid photo as new Maritime Senior Men's Curling Champions. They won the prestigious McLellan Cup on February 12, 1930.

Back row (l–r): M. G. "Mack" Goudge, G. V. "Judy" Smith, C. Logan "Logue" Smith, H. G. B. "Harold" Wilcox; front row: H. S. "Harold" Anslow, Andrew "Tobe" Mounce, G. P. "George" McIlheney, J. D. "Sherrif" Currie

PETE MILLS
AND CHILDREN,
SWIMMING ON
THE AVON RIVER
MUD FLATS,
1930S

The causeway built across the Avon River in 1970 ended swimming on the Avon River at the Water Street Beach. An open space between Rotundus Wharf and Shaw's Wharf was used for many years as a swimming beach during high tide. In the 1930s, the Playground Commission hired Pete Mills—shown here holding the hands of two young children—as a sports director. Pete was an all-round athlete of some stature in the Maritimes, and people greeted this move with pleasure. He had played ice hockey for the Truro Bearcats in the Nova Scotia Senior League, he played senior baseball, he was a boxer of note, and he was well versed in physical training. Swimming and diving, however, were his specialties. Upon his appointment he became involved in sport at all age levels. He played hockey and baseball for the town teams, taught boxing to youth and adults, and set up physical training in classrooms. The most thrilling thing for children was that he took over the Elmcroft Playgrounds and, with the assist-ance of volunteers, organized baseball and track-and-field programs. At the beach on Water Street he organized daily swimming classes for little ones. To teenagers he taught diving off of the wharf, as well as lifesaving courses. The program followed Red Cross instructional standards and certificates were issued for those who passed tests.

The water at the beach was always tinged brown with mud stirred up by the coming and going of the tide, but nobody seemed to mind, so great was the thrill of getting to swim. Aberdeen and Evangeline beaches were too far away for most children, so their attention was on the Water Street Beach.

Red Cross regulations required a rope with floats to be strung between the wharves overhanging the swimming area. Nobody was allowed out beyond the rope. Lifeguards were stationed, and the deep-voiced instructions of Pete Mills went a long way in keeping order. During playtime, as the tidal water was slowly creeping up the muddy slope, children were allowed to sit in the mud and slide into the water. The tempting mud ended up down the back of a few swimsuits.

Older children often found their ways to the river when the tide was out. They walked out to the centre of the riverbed, which was a beautiful sand bar. They could run and chase as well as swim in large puddles left in the sand, and there were muddy slopes to slide down into the channel also.

HELEN "HONEY" WOOD, APPLE BLOSSOM QUEEN, 1936

The Annapolis Valley Apple Blossom Festival began in 1932 under the direction of the Kentville Board of Trade. It was an immediate success, for with mayors of various Valley towns becoming involved in the planning, it had the support of the entire Valley population. Apple Blossom Sunday became an important day to travel through the Valley to see the beautiful orchards and photograph the blossoms.

"Princesses" were picked annually in each participating town, which assured support of the event from all parts of the Valley. Local and provincial newspapers ran photos of the candidates as excitement built during the week before the weekend festival at the height of the blossom spectacle. Knowing that each year an "Apple Blossom Queen" would be chosen from the participating princesses has maintained interest over the years. Traditionally, the pageant has been a very colourful display because of the originality and brilliance of the "Princess floats" used to show off the candidates during the Grand Parade preceding the crowning of the queen.

Windsor has had its fair share of queens over the years, beginning with Helen "Honey" Wood in 1936. Wood's nickname was suggestive of her personality and popularity in and around Windsor.

During the years of World War Two, interest in the festival heightened. Windsorians and people all over the province were excited about the choice of Christina Crowell at the height of the war in 1944, for she was a Sergeant in the Canadian Women's Army Corps. The military got to play a big role in the festival during the war years, all of which did much to heighten people's interest in the war effort as well as maintain enthusiasm for the Apple Blossom Festival.

In 1957, another popular Windsor candidate became blossom queen. Nancy Hughes took the honours and represented her home town in the fine tradition set by her predecessors, Honey and Teena. The latest queen from Windsor was Keri McAdoo in 1990.

WINDSOR'S SHARP SHOOTING RIFLE TEAM, 1936

This group of riflemen from Windsor began competing amongst themselves at a local rifle range by using 303 rifles from World War One. Soon they were competing provincially and found that they were able to win championships. They next formed a team that went to England to compete at Bisley, the British National Rifle Association competition, and won there also. In 1936, George V. "Judy" Smith, a well known all-round athlete from Windsor, was in charge of the local club and was a member of the council for the Nova Scotia Rifle Association. He led his contingent to a competition at the Bedford Rifle Range with wonderful results. This photo, taken at Bedford, shows the team and the amazing collection of trophies they won at that event.

L–r: George V. Smith (seated), Garwin Smith, his father Harold Smith, Lon King, Clarey Haley, Bill Sangster, Nando Davis, Earl Davis, Roy Mosher, Art Whalen

POND HOCKEY ON NESBITT'S ISLAND, 1940s

A field on Nesbitt's Island flooded and froze each winter to give children a place to play pond hockey. Even when an indoor rink became available in Windsor, most children could not afford to play inside. Pond hockey continued to flourish through the years of World War Two and beyond. The house in the background was the home of former shipbuilder Bennett Smith, whose busy shipyard in the mid- to late-nineteenth century was just beyond, on the edge of the Avon River.

**GEORGE R. WILEY,
1944**

In 1944, with World War Two at an end, folks turned their attention to creating a memorial to those brave people who had sacrificed their lives for our freedom. A Windsor gentleman named George Wiley, a recently deceased druggist, had had that on his mind as well. He left a condition in his will stating that if the people of Windsor would raise five thousand dollars toward a community centre, he would assign the residue of his estate to the construction and maintenance of a hall for young people of Windsor to participate in recreation, physical training, and education. People rose to his challenge and raised funds far beyond five thousand dollars. Adding Wiley's bequest to the amount raised, the Hants County War Memorial Centre became a reality. The youth of the entire county were granted facilities that met Mr. Wiley's prescribed standards, and which had not been available before.

ROTARIANS PARADE, 1950

Members of the Rotary Club have been noted for their fundraising abilities and worthy community projects over the years in Windsor. The Rotary Club was (and remains) an international service club. The Windsor branch raised funds to provide summer camp for children, build a community swimming pool, and other such good works. In particular, they have held an annual radio auction since the 1940s, when CFAB first appeared as a local radio station.

In 1950, the club had a parade that drew much attention from people for miles around. The streets were filled with folks in mob-proportions hoping to get a glimpse of some of the town's noted citizens dressed up in unbelievable costumes. The Rotarians made fools of themselves all in the name of good sportsmanship and community-minded fundraising.

The parade went from Victoria Park down Gerrish Street and Water Street, then back again, with Rotarians acting the clowns all the way. It was a cold, misty and muddy day but spirits ran high and everybody there seemed to have a delightful time as they supported the Rotarians and their community effort.

One photo shows a section of the parade stopped for a photo opportunity (l-r): Mayor Doug Morton, Ralph Parsons looking on, "Nurse-maid" Rhoda MacDonald, R. N., "Pediatric Nurse" Mellish Lane, T. B. Akin looking on, "Baby" Dr. Owen B. Keddy, and "Nanny with protective umbrella" Reg Giffin.

MARIE (SEXTON) DILL (L), 1956

The first time Marie (Sexton) Dill fell in love, it was with hockey! As a girl she began playing the game in Scotch Village, on ponds and the nearby flooded marsh. Only boys were playing hockey in the village, so she had to be strong, fast and defiant in order to stay in the game. Possessing all of those qualities, Dill quickly learned the thrill of scoring goals. Her father would cut wooden pucks for her from the woodpile in the backyard, and Dill yearned to play hockey every chance she had, usually after school and on Saturdays. Ralph O'Brien, who ran the country store in Scotch Village, knew of her hockey talents and drove her into town at age sixteen to arrange an introduction with the Windsor Girls' Hockey Team. A naturally jovial person, Dill fit in well and was accepted immediately by the Windsor team. She was excited to be involved in real games with teams from Kentville and Halifax, as opposed to pond hockey back in the village. Dill moved to town, got a job at Wier's Restaurant, and settled into playing for the Windsor Girls' Team. She became team captain the following season.

For two years, the Windsor Girls' Hockey Team was unbeaten in their many games. In both seasons, Dill played centre for Windsor and led in scoring for the entire Annapolis Valley. Her team scored sixty-one goals in the season of 1957–58, and Dill scored forty-five of them. She often played the entire game; if she felt tired, she would slide back on defence until she caught her breath, and then she would skate back to the forward line again.

**MARY MUNRO,
FAN SUPREME,
1962**

Mary Munro came to Windsor from Pictou County as a young woman in the 1920s and brought a love of people and of hockey with her. A mother of three hockey-playing children, she supported local teams as a fan for many years. Munro and a group of her friends loved to watch games in the old Stannus Street rink, where she had a favourite standing place: just inside the main door at the end of the rink, looking through the chicken wire behind the net, next to the goal judge. From that vantage point she could see everybody who entered and left the rink and the players as they went on and off the ice between periods. Mary knew and loved the game. One evening in 1962, she was surprised as the players honoured her with a presentation at centre ice. Ivan Tennant, a player with the Windsor Maple Leafs, is seen here presenting Munro with flowers as a sign of the players' appreciation for her many years of support.

Chapter 9

Special Events

LORD AND LADY ABERDEEN, 1894

ord Aberdeen of Scotland, the Governor General of Canada (1893–98), and Lady Aberdeen came to Windsor in 1894, and the town greeted them around a lavishly decorated elevated platform built alongside the station. This photo, taken by Lewis Rice, shows that people from miles around the shire-town of Hants County turned out for the occasion. A beach at nearby Mount Denson, long popular as a summer resort with Windsorians, was named Aberdeen Beach in their honour.

THE ROTUNDUS FERRY BOAT FOR WORK AND PLEASURE, 1912

This photo was taken on August 16, 1912, on the occasion of a visit to Windsor by the Governor General of Canada, the Duke of Connaught, and Princess Louise. Mayor Herbert W. Sangster arranged for a picnic cruise on the river in the midday sunshine for children and a few guardians. In a time before cars, television, or even many radios, this occasion would have been the height of excitement for the children. Free homemade vanilla ice cream was served on board that day.

On moonlit nights in summer, special evening trips out onto the river in the *Rotundus* were planned, with the Citizens Band on board to play waltzes and rousing military marches as entertainment for those couples taking advantage of the romantic moonlight excursions!

**PRINCE ARTHUR,
PRINCESS LOUISE
AND PRINCESS
PATRICIA, 1912**

**CHILDREN
SUSPENDED
IN MAYOR
SANGSTER'S
ARCH, 1912**

Governor General (1911-1916) Prince Arthur, the Duke of Connaught, visited Windsor with his wife, the Countess, Princess Louise, and their daughter, Princess Patricia. The date was August 16, 1912, and the visit was a very exciting and costly affair. The royal party was chauffeured through the decorated streets of town to Victoria Park for a general reception. Next they were paraded toward King's College, where the Duke was granted an honorary degree. The many exquisite arches built over the streets for the parade were lavish in their construction. The most remarkable was the mayor's arch, which stood across the street in front of Mayor H. B. Sangster's home on Vinegar Hill. Suspended from the arch were five small ropeswings, each containing a beautifully dressed child.

DOMINION DAY PARADE, 1920

In this photo, gloriously decorated horse-drawn wagon floats, interspersed with a few car and truck floats, are proceeding from the north end of Water Street toward Albert Street. The first float in the line shows a four-horse team and a model of Windsor's first hothouse. Next is an open-bodied truck, one of the first of its type to be invented. It has large decorative "running lamps," just like those used on wagons for night travel. Beyond that point are more wagons, decorated cars and people in fancy dress, and top hats, walking.

Community parades brought Windsorians together several times a year. Beginning with the parade of farmers and animals to the first Windsor Exhibition in 1756, the town's people seemed to use every opportunity to celebrate with a parade. Confederation in 1867 gave those who desired it an opportunity to celebrate Dominion Day every first of July. Empire Day was celebrated prior to Queen Victoria's Golden Jubilee in 1897, when it was changed to Victoria Day.

Huge crowds are present in old photographs of parades, showing that they were exciting events for the citizens of Windsor.

NORTH AMERICA'S OLDEST COUNTRY FAIR, 1920S

In 1765, Fort Edward became the site of the first agricultural fair in the colony of Nova Scotia and North America. The fair has changed names over the years but is still in existence, making it the longest running agricultural fair in North America.

Businesses in Halifax offered prizes and awards for the owners of the animals and vegetables judged to be "Best of Show." Every September, regional farmers showed their best animals and agricultural products at the fair. Gradually, the fair became known as the Windsor Exhibition. In the 1940s, as it came to involve farms over the whole county, the name changed to The Hants County Exhibition.

From the beginning, special barns and sheds were constructed on Fort Edward so that animals and fowl could be cared for during Exhibition week. Farmers stayed with their animals overnight during the entire time of the fair and eventually led them away from Fort Hill and home over town streets and country roads, showing off winners' red, blue, and white ribbons as the annual fair ended. In more recent years, with the institution of the 4-H Club, children began participating in the showing of animals and produce. As well, displays of work done in school have been exhibited, adding to the interest of children and their families. An exciting part of the fair has always been the tests of strength of animals, like the ox-pull and the horse-pull, in which teams of animals compete by pulling a sled loaded with boxes of sand of standard weight. Over the years, other features of competition and entertainment have been added to the fair.

In the 1960s the fair grounds were changed from Windsor's oldest military site to its newest—from Fort Edward to the site on Wentworth Road that had been the home of the Acadia Barracks during World War Two.

GWVA PARADE, 1923

The Veterans who returned to Canada following World War One formed an association called the Great War Veterans Association (GWVA). Members were also members of the larger association known as the British Empire Service League (BESL). The Windsor-Hants County Branch headquarters was in the Knights of Pythias (K of P) Hall on Gerrish Street. The K of P was dedicated to promoting peace and goodwill to all humanity. Having both organizations use the same building was a natural union. The K of P had the downstairs space and the GWVA used the second-storey rooms. They began having regular meetings and a special week of celebration during the week of November 11th, which they designated Armistice Week. That included a march to the new cenotaph at Victoria Park for a memorial service.

This photo shows the membership marching away from their headquarters, led by Captain Gerald McIlhenny, with Sergeant Jim Weatherbed bringing up the rear. Both these gentlemen had been decorated for gallant service in Europe.

Other veterans included in the photograph are Baxter Fulton, Everett Knowles, Percy Kilcup, Milford Dimock, Andrew "Tobe" Mounce, Chester Smith, and Earl Kuhn. Here they are marching beneath an arch at the corner of Grey and Gerrish streets, on their way to Victoria Park. Veterans unable to walk were driven in automobiles that followed the marchers. Crowds of people filled the streets when these memorial services were first organized.

**THE CIRCUS
ARRIVES, 1935**

Having the railway run through the central streets of town paid off whenever the circus arrived. Here the Barnes Circus crew is seen unloading wagons and animals from the train used to carry them from town to town. The train merely stopped in its tracks, so to speak, and the circus rolled off toward the Athletic Grounds, near the station where the big top was pitched for the three-ring circus later the same day. Of course, there was a circus parade through the streets as soon as things were set up. Large posters, like those shown in the ice cream parlour window, were plastered over sides of buildings and store windows for weeks beforehand in preparation for the "Biggest Show On Earth!"

BILLY BISHOP'S PLANE, 1939

Just after supper hour on a warm summer evening in June 1939, the unfamiliar sound of an airplane was heard circling Windsor. It caught the immediate attention of everybody around, for the sound and sight of an aircraft was a complete oddity to all in town but one. Francis Clarke, who was a member of the peacetime Air Force, just happened to be home on holiday from Ottawa, where he was stationed. When the Grumman Goose craft came in low and glided onto the shallow brown water of the Avon River, Francis was one of the first to be alerted and to appear at Shaw's Wharf, where the plane taxied before cutting its twin motors. The crew threw lines ashore, which willing onlookers tied to the docks. They waited for the tide to recede before the crew could go ashore and reveal the purpose of the visit. By then, to their surprise, the bared shore was found to be deep and slippery mud. The first footprints were made by the pilot, followed by the co-pilot, and next by their very distinguished passenger, World War One (or Great War, at that time) Canadian flying ace, Billy Bishop. He had been in Halifax attending to official business and was being flown back to Air Force headquarters in Ottawa when the pilot perceived a minor engine problem that made him decide to come in for a landing and check out the system. The crew members made their way across Water Street, where they were met by Francis Clarke, with whom they conferred. Inside Peter MacKinnon's garage, two decisions were made. Peter and the crew would check the engine, and Bishop and his crew would stay overnight at the nearby Victoria Hotel. With the tide receding to the Bay of Fundy for eleven hours, there was no chance of an earlier takeoff anyway. Most of the people in town and county stopped by the waterfront throughout the evening to marvel at the sight of the Grumman Goose stuck in the Avon River mud. As day dawned and the tide returned on time, so did the crew. Clarke, whose vacation leave was nearly ended anyway, decided to hitch a free flight back to base with the others. Once the plane floated above the mud flats, the engines were tested, lines thrown overboard, and the craft set adrift. Setting the engines in reverse for a couple of minutes backed the aircraft from between the old wharves into the river's stream, then, turning, the pilot taxied southward to prepare for takeoff. He stopped short of the highway bridge and turned north into the wind. What excitement as the engines sped up to maximum and then took the plane quickly downstream and smoothly off of the water into the sky, with muddy water slipping away in the airstream. Everybody was waving and watching in amazement one of the town's most exciting events.

THE MIDWAY AT THE HANTS COUNTY EXHIBITION, 1943

Over the years, the Exhibition on Fort Edward featured the musical rides of the Bill Lynch Show. Customarily, school was closed on Tuesday, as it was "Children's Day" at the exhibition. Rides on the merry-go-round, ferris wheel, whip, and caterpillar were offered at half price to allow children to enjoy the fun of the fair. Canvas tents were set up with awnings that allowed folks to be protected from rain as they played games of skill in hopes of winning a celluloid doll or toy. Other tents were used for side shows, in which customers could view what were unfortunately billed as "freaks of nature"—midgets, giants, two-headed animals, and oddly shaped vegetables.

OPENING OF HALIBURTON MEMORIAL MUSEUM, 1940

Sir Wylie Greer, who painted the portrait of T.C. Haliburton on the easel, is shown standing on a platform in front of the entrance to Sam Slick's house. He is addressing the crowd at the official opening of the Haliburton Memorial Museum on July 4, 1940. To the right are mayor of Windsor, Ira B. Lohnes, Minister of Highways and Public Works, A.S. MacMillan, and Windsor photographer Harry Reid.

GOVERNOR GENERAL LORD BYNG OF VIMY, 1926

Lord Byng became Governor General in 1921 but was well known to Canadians ever since he led the Canadian Army to victory at Vimy Ridge in 1916. A 1926 visit to Windsor by Lord Byng of Vimy was a welcome event. He reviewed the returned soldiers of Hants County at the DAR station, as shown in this photo. With him is Col. Hedley Tremaine, who had been the commanding officer of the 112th Regiment from Windsor. The town's dignitaries were there in morning dress to meet the Governor General. Councillor Joey Mortimer and other dignitaries are seen speaking with the crowd in the background.

THE WINDSOR CONCERT PARTY, 1945

Throughout World War Two, the variety show was the most exciting live form of entertainment in the entire nation. Thousands of young army, navy, and air force troops across Canada needed leisure-time fun. The Windsor Concert Party was a fine example of the efforts other Canadians made to provide that fun. Within months of the arrival of troops in Windsor, a group of dedicated people formed a program of delightful song-and-dance routines that was an instant success with both the armed forces and civilians.

When the first program was ready, it was tested on the public before it headed for service bases. The *Hants Journal* advertised, the Imperial Theatre hosted, and excited Windsorians enjoyed the show before it went on the road. All three shows played to packed houses (510, including balcony) and paved the way to success for the talented volunteer participants. Any profit went to supplying the extravagant costumes that added so much to the production.

After thrilling the local audience, the Concert Party headed out for evening performances at service depots and wherever else they were needed to keep spirits riding high in a country at war. When the final curtain came down on the 1945 shows, people rejoiced at the end of the war but were saddened to have their long-running series of magnificent variety shows come to an end.

Windsor Concert Party, 1945

Back row (l–r): Charlie Walker, Florence Wood, Tobe Mounce, Dorothy Brown, Tom White, Rita Sherman, Blaine Smith, Conrad Taylor, Sterling Edwards, Burton Caldwell, Don Holmes, Percy "Bud" White, Jim Regan, Bob Reid, Willard Bishop, Frank Harview, Jim Campbell, Bob Paulin, Marion Moore, Bill Underwood, K. Caldwell, Hilda Philpott, Marguerite Eagles, E. L. Eagles, Kay Knowles, Johnny Hughes; middle row: Doug Atkinson, Kay Anslow, Bob Reid; front row: Jean Singer, Gerry Aylward, E. Fairbairn, Jean Reid, Mary Shankel, Nancy Blanchard

Andrea Stephens, daughter of fire chief Walter Stephens and Alison Stephens, is shown here after making a presentation to Governor General Vincent Massey at Victoria Park. Massey also visited King's College School and the Haliburton Memorial Museum during the 1957 visit.

The Honourable Vincent Massey was born in Canada and was the first Canadian appointed to the office of Governor General. He was a brother of noted actor Raymond Massey and son of the president of the Massey–Harris Company, manufacturer of farm machinery. He studied at Oxford University prior to becoming a professor of English at Victoria University in Toronto in 1915. As Governor General from 1952–59, he visited all parts of Canada and did much to promote the arts, leading to the creation of the National Library of Canada and the Canada Council. His energetic support of the humanities in Canada led to the formation of the Massey Lectures in his honour. The people of Windsor were delighted to welcome him to their town.

Bibliography

Aylward, Thomas and Anne Hutten. *As Days Go By*. Hantsport, NS: Lancelot Press, 1983.

Blanchard, H. Percy. "I Remember (Stories of Windsor)," [series] in *The Hants Journal*, 1930.

Board of Trade. "Windsor Nova Scotia." [Booklet] Windsor: 1923.

Bruce, Harry. *Illustrated History of Nova Scotia*. Halifax: Nimbus Publishing, 1997.

Centennial Committee, The. "Gateway to the Valley." [High school students' project] Windsor: December 1977.

Clarke, W. W. *Clarke's History of the Earliest Railways in Nova Scotia*. Windsor: The Hants Journal Press, 1920.

Davies, Richard A., ed. *The Haliburton Bi-centenary Chaplet: The 1996 Thomas Raddall Symposium*. Kentville: Gaspereau Press, 1997

Duncanson, John V. *Falmouth: A New England Township in Nova Scotia, 1760–1965*.

Herbin, John Frederic. *The History of Grande Pré by The Only Descendant of the Exiled People Who Lived in The Grand-Pré of the Acadians*. Kentville: Gaspereau Press, 2003. First published 1898 by Barnes & Co. in Saint John.

Hind, Henry Youle. *An Early History of Windsor, Nova Scotia*. Hantsport, NS: Lancelot Press, 1989. First published 1889 by Jas. J. Anslow, at *The Hants Journal* office. -

Jones, George P. *Windsor: Its History, Points of Interest, and Representative Business Men*. Windsor: J. J. Anslow, 1893.

Loomer, L. S. *Windsor, Nova Scotia: a journey in history*. Kentville: West Hants Historical Society/Gaspereau Press, 1996.

Paul, Daniel L. *We Were Not The Savages*. Halifax: Nimbus Publishing, 1993.

Pope, William. "Portrait of Windsor: the Wonderful World of Windsor, N. S." Self published booklet, c.1960s.

Robertson, Barbara R. *Gingerbread & House Finish of Every Description*. Halifax: Nova Scotia Museum, 1990.

Shand, Gwendolyn Vaughan. *Historic Hants County*. Halifax: McCurdy Printing Company, 1979

Vroom, Frederick Williams. "Memories of Windsor in the Seventies," [series] in *The Hants Journal*, January 27 and February 3, 1932.

Watts, Heather. *Silent Steeds: Cycling in Nova Scotia to 1900*. Halifax: Nova Scotia Museum, 1985.

Whitehead, Ruth Holmes. *The Old Man Told Us*. Halifax: Nimbus Publishing, 1991.

Woodworth, Marguerite. *History of the Dominion Atlantic Railway*. Kentville: Kentville Publishing Company, 1936.

Photo Credits

Acadia University: 104b
Anslow, Kay: 26, 50, 82, 112, 120, 125, 134a, 153
Bain, Saundra (Smith): 109
Bishop, Diana: 80
Bishop, Eileen: 114, 136
Bishop, Jean (Reid): 122
Bremner, Jim: 65, 115
Cochrane, Edmund: 70
Cochrane, Gary: 73
Dill, Howard: 142
Dill, Marie: 141
Fogarty, Harry: 121
Garth Vaughan/James Valentine Postcard Collection: 7, 12, 51b, 55, 72, 91, 92
Garth Vaughan Collection: 3, 4, 6, 8a, 8b, 10, 18, 19, 20a, 20b, 21, 23, 25,
28a, 28b, 29, 30b, 43, 44b, 48, 49, 51a, 52, 53, 63, 64, 66, 67, 71, 80, 87, 88,
89, 93, 96, 97, 98, 99, 107, 119, 123, 127, 128, 131, 132, 135, 137a, 137b,
139, 146, 148, 151
Gwendolyn Vaughan Shand Collection: 9
Herbin, Chris: 116
Huggins, Jack: 124
Imperial Oil Collection: 103
Lancelot Press: 5
MacKinnon, Peter: 83, 84b, 86, 152
Nova Scotia Archives and Records Management: 101
Nova Scotia Museum: 16
O'Rourke, Olive: 61, 78
Patterson, Brenda: 149
Patterson, Saint Clair: 118
Riley, Vivian: 100a
Robinson, Ada: 113
Siderius, Lilla: 85
Smith, Gilbert: 84a
Smith, Richard: 59
Smith, Sid: 137
Smith, Virginia (Shand): 68, 69, 18a, 111a, 111b, 126
Stephens, Walter: 35, 36, 95, 154
Strum, David: 110b
Sweet, George: 74, 138
Taylor, Richard: 100b
Taylor, Ruth: 144, 145a, 145b
Vaughan, Lauren (Dougall): 58
Walker, Shirley: 76
West Hants Historical Society: i, 1, 11, 13, 14a. 14b, 15, 17, 22, 24, 27a, 27b,
30a, 31, 37a, 37b, 38, 39a, 40b, 41, 44a, 45, 46a, 46b, 47, 54, 56, 57, 62, 75,
77, 79, 94, 105, 106, 130 (Reid Studio), 134b (Reid Studio), 140, 143, 149
(Hants Journal), 152a, 152b
Wilcox, Helen: 90
Wilcox, Jim: 108b
Windsor Fire Department Museum: 35, 36, 41b, 42a